Revised Edition

KNOWLEDGE WHIZZ 5

Kunal Savarkar   Seema Chari

Collins

KNOWLEDGE WHIZZ 5

Revised Edition

Kunal Savarkar • Seema Chari

Published by Collins India
A division of HarperCollins*Publishers* India Private Limited

HarperCollins *Publishers*
A-75, Sector 57, Noida, Uttar Pradesh 201301, India

1 London Bridge Street, London SE1 9GF, United Kingdom

2 Bloor Street East, Toronto, Ontario M4W 1A8, Canada

Lvl 13, 201 Elizabeth Street (PO Box A565, NSW, 1235), Sydney NSW 2000, Australia

195 Broadway, New York, NY 10007, USA

Browse the complete Collins catalogue at **www.collins.in**

First published in 2016
Latest revised edition 2018

Reprint: 10 9 8 7 6 5 4 3 2 1

ISBN: 978-93-5264-553-4

Content designed by
Henu Studio Private Limited

Content developed by
Xpress Minds Edutainment Pvt. Ltd.

Artwork and layout by
Henu Studio Private Limited

Printed and bound by MicroPrints India, New Delhi

Acknowledgements

Cover: Henu Studio Pvt. Ltd.
Ishvaaku; Mcasankar; Mayank1704

Inside: p9: Parliament-GettyImages/Hindustan Times; Team-GettyImages/JOHN PRYKE AFP; Parcel-istock/wragg; Flight-istock/Nomadsoul1; Run-istock/GlobalStock; Ra -istock/Sportstock; Bouquet-istock/marilyna; Kettle-istock/worac; Building-istock/Deejpilot; Wrist Watch-stock/yogesh_more; Hedge-GettyImages/Benjamin Rondel Photonica; Cast-GettyImages/John O'Loughlin Moment; **p10:** Challenger Deep, Mariana Trench-corbisimages/ NASA/Corbis; Caspian Sea Map-istock/200mm; Death Valley-istock/sphraner; Antarcticaistock/Marc-Andre_LeTourneux; Amazon River-istock/Phototreat; **p11:** Northeast Greenland National Park-corbisimages/Radius Images/Corbis; Map of Antarctica-istock/duncan1890; Mawsynram-GettyImages/ROBERTO SCHMIDT; Angel Falls-istock/macbibi; Congo Riveristock/ Guenter Guni; **p18:** Indian State Outlines-Collins Bartholomew Ltd 2015; Howrah Bridge-GettyImages/Tuul and Bruno Morandi; Olive Ridley Sea Turtles-GettyImages/Photo Researchers Science Source; Nalanda-GettyImages/De Agostini; Jonha Falls-Wikipedia/Binayrungta; **p19:** Indian State Outlines-Collins Bartholomew Ltd 2015; Satyajit Ray-GettyImages/ULLSTEIN BILD; Rabindranath Tagore-GettyImages/Hulton Archive; Netaji Subhash Chandra Bose-GettyImages/Exotica.im; Madhubani Painting-GettyImages/Exotica.im; Santhal Group-GettyImages/SUBHENDU SARKAR; Gopalpur Beach-GettyImages/MARKA; **p29:** Real-istock/alexsl; Yuan-istock/Nikada; Rouble-GettyImages/ULLSTEIN BILD; Randistock/RapidEye; Ringgit-GettyImages/ULLSTEIN BILD; Euro-istock/acilo; **p30:** Portuguese Flag-istock/alexsl; Turkish Flag-istock/JJMaree; Russian Flag-istock/alexsl; Swiss Flag-istock/liangpv; Japanese Flag-istock/chokkicx; Arabian Flag-istock/Mybona; **p31:** kpalimski; RedHelga; Amarita; volofin; Talaj; al62; 3drenderings; ivkuzmin; malerapaso; foto-ianniello; mustafagull; sergeyryzhov; **p38:** Enid Blyton-GettyImages/ULLSTEIN BILD; Arthur Conan Doyle-GettyImages/Imagno; William Shakespeare-GettyImages/Print Collector; Charles Dickens-GettyImages/Stock Montage; Agatha Christie-GettyImages/Popperfoto; JK Rowling-GettyImages/Nomi Ellenson; **p39:** Wimbledon-GettyImages/ULLSTEIN BILD; eames-istock/meldayus; Buckingham Palace-istock/mikeinlondon; Baker Street Sign-istock/konstantin32; Big Ben- GettyImages/Alan Copson; Madame Tussaud's-istock/Marcus Lindstrom; King's Cross Station-GettyImages/Dan Kitwood; Tower Bridge-GettyImages/Daniel Viñé Garcia Moment; eTube-istock/Yuri_Arcurs; Lord's Cricket Ground-GettyImages/Mike Hewitt; **p46:** Dolphin-istock/beyhes; Hippopotamus-istock/Heatherfaye; Penguin-istock/AndreAnita; Jelly Fish-istock/cristianl; Seal-istock/Holger Mette; Star Fish-istock/Mutlu Kurtbas; Octopus-istock/Subaqueosshutterbug; Reindeer-istock/RolfAasa; Lizard Running on Water-GettyImages-Joe McDonald Visuals Unlimited; **p49:** Collins Bartholomew Ltd 2015; Akash Banerjee Photography; RNMitra; **p51:** Map of India-Collins Bartholomew Ltd 2015; **p53:** Tasmanian Tiger-istock/7activestudio; Passenger Pigeon-istock/nicolasprimola; Dodo-istock/Aunt_Spray; eGreat Auk-GettyImages/Hulton Archive; **p54:** Playground-istock/Mark Bowden; Rising Sun-istock/Porntep-Kawjun; Tulips-istock/bluestocking; Sugar Bowl-istock/thumb; White Elephant-istock/davincidig; underbolt-istock/Maxiphoto; Rainbow-istock/Preto_perola; Maple Leaf-istock/Marek Mnich; Long White Cloud-istock/gong hangxu; Gi -istock/ProjectB; **p55:** Brazil Flag Map-istock/scibak; Pele-GettyImages/Martin Bernetti; Christ the Redeemer-GettyImages/Plastock; Co ee-istock/mariusFM77; Piranha-istock/alexeys; football-istock/forest_strider; **p56:** Labrador-istock/Bigandt_Photography; Poodle-istock/ultramarinfoto; Pug-istock/Lexi eMonster; Golden Retriever-istock/Bigandt_Photography; **p57:** Pomeranian-istock/swaite; Dalmatian-istock/fotojagodka; German Shepherd-istock/Koljambus; St. Bernard-istock/tobkatrina; **p64:** Don Bradman-GettyImages/Hulton Archive; Tiger Woods-GettyImages/Timothy Clary; Mohammad Ali-GettyImages-ULLSTEIN BILD; Michael Phelps-GettyImages/ULLSTEIN BILD; Nadia Comaneci-GettyImages/Daniel Zuchnik WireImage; **p65:** Michael Jordan-GettyImages/Jason Merritt; Pele-GettyImages/Martin Bernetti; Jesse Owens-GettyImages/ULLSTEIN BILD; Dhyan Chand-static.sportskeeda.com; Martina Navratilova-GettyImages/ULLSTEIN BILD; **p66:** Cave Painting-istock/bortonia; Ajanta Painting-GettyImages/IndiaPictures; Miniature-GettyImages/Universal History Archive; Rajasthan-GettyImages/Exotica.im; Pahari-GettyImages/Indian School Art Images; Raja Ravi Varma's Painting-GettyImages/IndiaPictures; **p67:** Self Portrait of Amrita Sher-Gil-GettyImages/BEN STANSALL; Kalighat Painting-GettyImages/IndiaPictures; MF Hussain Painting-GettyImages/CHRIS JACKSON; Tanjore-GettyImages/De Agostini; Madhubani-GettyImages/Exotica.im; **p68:** India Post-GettyImages/Frank Bienewald; Aero ot-GettyImages/ULLSTEIN BILD; Maersk-GettyImages/Bloomberg; ai Airlines- GettyImages/Bloomberg; United Airlines-GettyImages/MIRA OBERMAN AFP; Amtrak-GettyImages/George Rose; Cathay Paci c-aviationguide.net; Air France-GettyIma

Preface

Welcome to ***Knowledge Whizz*** Version 2.0! Our belief that knowledge is for everyone has resonated well across the country, with thousands of school children now using the series, thereby reinforcing our conviction that general knowledge is not the exclusive preserve of a few quizzers. In this multimedia age, knowledge is everywhere, but sourcing, assimilating and recalling it is a skill that can be learned!

Knowledge Whizz, now in its second edition, is a unique series that aims to offer general knowledge covering a wide range of subjects, both curricular as well as extra-curricular, to children from six to thirteen years of age. These are GK books for learning, not quiz books for testing.

Salient features of the series

- Each task comprises at least two kinds of inputs to help children arrive at the answers and acquire knowledge at the same time.
- Tasks cover a wide range of topics presented with a twist. For instance, history includes the story of the automobile, bicycle, cinema, cricket and flight; science includes accidental inventions and discoveries; geography comes alive through associative information and culturally rich chapters. Language and literature cover trivia and etymology, two wonderful learning tools.
- Themes from modern life such as gaming, media, business and finance are extensively explored as well as tidbits about the quirky and the quotidian.
- **India-specific content** presented beautifully through fun, richly illustrated tasks, designed to whet the curiosity of children and inspire them to explore their beautiful country in all its diversity. New chapters on **North East India** bring the vibrancy and uniqueness of this relatively lesser known part of India to children everywhere.
- The books do not expect children to be pre-equipped with knowledge but instead reward inquisitiveness by giving them workoutable tasks.
- The artistic and colourful layouts make the presentation more accessible, exciting and alluring whilst facilitating self-learning.
- Special features are an exciting mixed bag of environment education, life skills, values, quick quizzes, cool facts, cool activity, evaluation of multiple intelligences and Higher Order Thinking Skills to make children become well-rounded individuals.
- Brand new features incorporated into Version 2.0 include **Aptitudes**, aiming to hone and cement specific verbal, visual and logical aptitudes through the common lens of general knowledge, **Safety Science**, which draws our attention to the science behind the measures we should take to stay safe wherever we are, and **Game**, to bring a good dose of fun into learning.

We gratefully acknowledge the contribution of the Xpress Minds Edutainment team, whose inputs have been invaluable for this second edition.

We are certain that this series will open up the world of general knowledge and make learning a fun, instinctive and rewarding process for all.

~ Kunal Savarkar and Seema Chari

In This Book ...

Cooking with the Five Senses

A. Match the dishes with their descriptions. Also write the name of the dish in the space provided.

1.

____

a. salty rice dish cooked with vegetables and whole spices

b. salty flatbread, with a filling of mashed vegetables

2.

____

Multiple Intelligence tasks focus on the 8 Intelligences: interpersonal, intrapersonal, bodily kinesthetic, visual-spatial, logical reasoning, verbal-linguistic, naturalistic and musical. Each page explores 5-6 intelligences to encourage learners to learn in their own way and is not to be used for assessment.

Higher Order Thinking Skills (HOTS) pages encourage critical thinking and teach learners to analyse and evaluate information. Cool quizmaster, Kunal Savarkar, helps students become knowledge detectives and skilled quizzers.

PIN Codes

When you write an address in India, you would realize it normally ends with a six-digit number. This is the Postal Index Number or PIN Code. The PIN code on a letter or package helps a postman to deliver letters to the correct place in India.

A. Let us understand what these numbers mean, by taking a real example, 211001.

Cool Activity
Fun activities to learn through doing.

Cool Quiz
Encourages research to find solutions.

Current Affairs
Visit **www.collins.in/knowledgewhizz** for Current Affairs updates and weekly quizzes.

Behaviour in Public Places

Knowledge is important, but there is no substitute for good manners and etiquette. Read the following statements about behaviour in public places. Mark examples of good manners with a ☺ and bad manners with a ☹.

Values pages focus on inculcating values, morals, ethics and right attitudes in students through to-do tasks.

Life Skills pages expose learners to problems in real-life situations to help them learn to take decisions.

Reading Traffic Signs

A. *Each description below matches ONE of the two traffic signs shown. Tick (✓) the sign that matches the description. One has been done for you.*

Aptitude

Aptitude Tasks are designed to teach children to develop specific skills such as sequencing, classification, analogies and others through rebuses, matching, sorting and pattern activities, with step-by-step tips on how to solve them.

COOL FACT

William Shakespeare is believed to have been born on April 23, 1564. He was baptised on April 26 that year. Interestingly, he died on April 23, 1616.

Green Earth

Green Earth page focuses on environmental issues and imbibes the right attitude towards conservation of environment.

COOL FACT

Factoids linked to the content of the page. The fun element in them will make you say, 'Hey! Cool to know that.'

Safety Science

Safety is not just a notion; it is a science, which means it is guided by research, facts and figures. From home to school, public places to controlled environments, we can do a lot to keep ourselves safe. The Safety Science chapters in each book show us how.

Game

Life is a game! Each book in the series has at least one puzzle, maze or strategy-based activity, always with a GK twist, but with the added feel-good incentive of "winning the game".

Quiz Yourself are quick quizzes to assess what the children have learned in the book. The main themes and the cool facts will all form the basis of the Quiz Yourself section, intended as a self-evaluation tool from books 3 to 8.

Detailed Contents

Natural World

A Flock of Birds
Animals Adapt
Dramatic Nature
Extinct Animals
Man's Best Friend
Move Like an Animal
Super Birds

Logical Reasoning

What Is to What?

Language and Literature

Colourful Expressions
Words from Shakespeare
The Fantasy World of Roald Dahl

Entertainment

Cartoon Connections

Around the World

Earth Extremes
Interesting Jobs
Money Exchange
Let's Visit the UK
Sobriquets for Countries
Let's Visit Brazil
Different Kinds of Boats
Let's Visit Pakistan

Science

Chocolate
Technology Decoded
Manufacturing Fruit Juice
Freaky Inventions

Sports

All Time Greats in Sports
Rules of the Game
Olympic Symbols

Art

Wonders of the Ancient World
Indian Paintings

India

Let's Go East
Hill Stations
Indian Brides and Grooms
Nature's Bounty in North East India
Puppets
Traditional Musical Instruments of India

Trivia

Symbols in Computers

History

How Did Humans Fly?
The Story of Cricket

Safety Science

Safety During Celebrations

Mixed Bag

Multiple Intelligences	Cooking with the Five Senses
Life Skill	Reading Traffic Signs
Value	Behaviour in Public Places
Green Earth	Different Kinds of Wastes
HOTS	PIN Codes State and Vehicle Codes
Game	Game of the World
Aptitude	Happy New year Countries Linked to Words Types of Doctors Internet Country Codes The Number 5 Airlines and Logos

Quiz Yourself

Keys

Contents

1. A Flock of Birds	9
2. Earth Extremes	10
3. Cartoon Connections	12
4. Interesting Jobs	14
Cooking with the Five Senses	16
5. Let's Go East	18
6. Colourful Expressions	20
7. Words from Shakespeare	21
Happy New Year	22
Reading Traffic Signs	23
8. Chocolate	24
9. Hill Stations	26
10. Wonders of the Ancient World	28
11. Money Exchange	29
Countries Linked to Words	30
14. Dramatic Nature!	32
15. Indian Brides and Grooms	34
16. Manufacturing Fruit Juice	36
17. Let's Visit the UK	38
Game of the World	40
Behaviour in Public Places	42
Types of Doctors	44
12. Animals Adapt	46
The Number 5	47
19. Nature's Bounty in North East India	48
Internet Country Codes	49
PIN Codes	50
20 Extinct Animals	52
21 Sobriquets for Countries	54
22 Let's Visit Brazil	55
23 Man's Best Friend	56
Different Kinds of Waste	58
24 How Did Humans Fly?	60
25 Puppets	62
26 All Time Greats in Sports	64
27 Indian Paintings	66
Airlines and Logos	68
13 Technology Decoded	69
28 Different Kinds of Boats	70
29 Move Like an Animal	71
30 Safety During Celebrations	72
31 Super Birds	74
32 Traditional Musical Instruments of India	75
33 Let's Visit Pakistan	76
34 Rules of the Game	78
35 The Story of Cricket	80
36 Freaky Inventions	82
37 The Fantasy World of Roald Dahl	84
38 What Is to What?	85
State and Vehicle Codes	86
39 Olympic Symbols	88
40 Symbols in Computers	90
Quiz Yourself	91
Keys	

1

A Flock of Birds

Groups of birds have very interesting and unusual names. Use the picture clue and the help box to guess the group name for different birds.

bouquet	watch	raft	team	parcel	parliament
flight	run	hedge	cast	building	kettle

1. 

a ____________ of owls

2. 

a ____________ of ducks

3. 

a ____________ of penguins

4. 

a ____________ of pigeons

5. 

a ____________ of poultry

6. 

a ____________ of coots

a ____________ of pheasants

a ____________ of hawks

9. 

a ____________ of rooks

10. 

a ____________ of nightingales

11. 

a ____________ of herons

12. 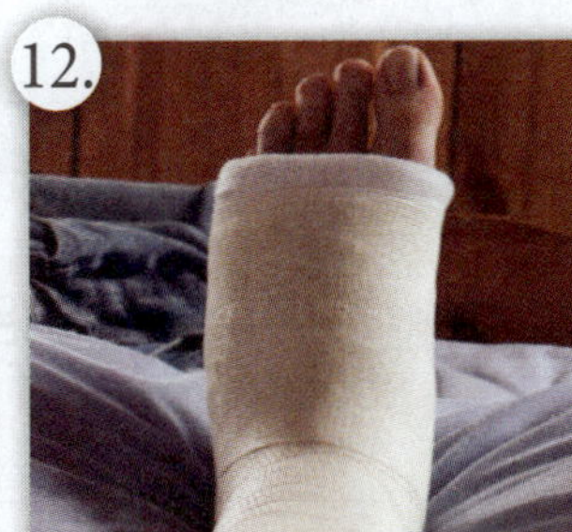

a ____________ of falcons

COOL FACT

Here are three more interesting names. Find more for fun!

- a murder of crows
- a screech of gulls
- a riot of robins

AROUND THE WORLD

2

Earth Extremes

Fill in the blanks about the deepest, highest, hottest, coldest and other extreme realities on Earth. Use the words from the help box. But watch out! There are some extra answers.

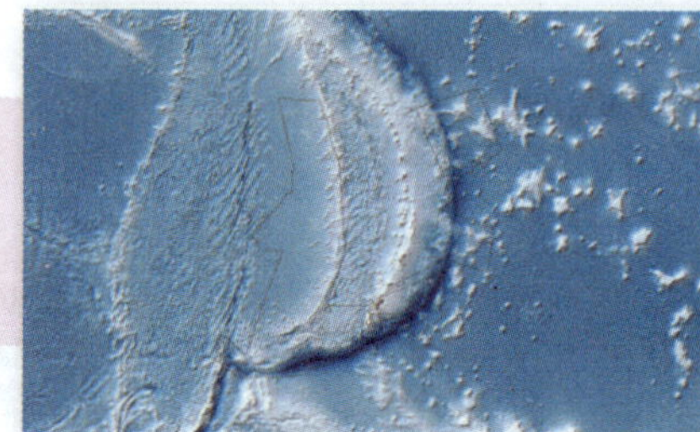

1. Challenger Deep, the deepest point on Earth, is located within the __________ __________.

2. With a surface area of more than 370,000 sq km __________ __________ is the world's largest lake.

3. The hottest natural temperature of 56.7°C was recorded on 10 July, 1913 at __________ __________.

4. Situated more than 1,700 kilometres away from the nearest landmass, ____________, Bouvet Island is considered to be the remotest place on Earth.

5. With discharges of about 209,000 m^3 (7,380,765 cubic feet) of water every second, ____________ is the largest river in the world.

COOL FACT Hawaii's Mauna Kea is only 4,205 metres above sea level. If it is measured from the sea-floor, the mountain rises about 9,966 metres. So, in a way, it is the world's tallest mountain.

6. Covering an area of 972,000 km^2, __________ __________ National Park is the largest and most northerly one in the world.

7. In 2010, the temperature near __________ __________, Antarctica dipped to −93.0°C, making it the coldest place on Earth.

8. Receiving an average annual rainfall of 11,873 mm, __________ in Meghalaya, is the rainiest place in the world.

9. At a height of 979 metres, __________ Falls is the world's highest uninterrupted waterfall.

10. Reaching depths of 220 metres in its lower course, the __________ is the deepest river in the world.

Death Valley | Vostok Station | Amazon | Antarctica
Caspian Sea | Northeast Greenland | Congo | Nile
Mawsynram | Mariana Trench | Australia | Angel

ENTERTAINMENT

3

Cartoon Connections

Here are some characters from famous comic series. The characters given in each box, that is, Box 1 and Box 2, have a connection, given in the Connection Box. Choose a character from each of the boxes and the connection they share and write in the table given on the next page. One has been done for you.

Box 1

Connection Box

a.	sailors	b.	gives superhuman strength
c.	ghostly trio from casper	d.	heroes from outer space
e.	Peanuts	f.	favourite food
g.	his 'wild' pet	h.	Laurel and Hardy

Box 2

i.

Sabu

ii.

Fatso

iii.

Captain Haddock

iv.

a plate of lasagna

v.

Snoopy

vi.

Stan

vii.

Cheetah

viii.

spinach

COOL FACT

Two of the most-loved comic book characters, enjoyed by children and adults, are Tintin and Asterix. Both these series were originally written in French and then translated into different languages.

Box 1	Connection	Box 2
1	a	iii

4

Interesting Jobs

Read the descriptions of some interesting professions and find them in the word search.

S	C	U	B	A	D	I	V	E	R	R	T
U	L	P	U	R	J	O	T	A	B	N	Q
N	O	E	T	T	H	A	S	S	E	E	U
N	W	R	T	I	K	C	E	T	S	S	I
Y	N	C	E	S	B	T	B	M	T	S	Z
R	A	A	S	T	R	O	N	A	U	T	M
A	C	R	R	O	E	R	L	G	N	A	A
I	K	T	L	O	Z	U	P	I	D	D	S
S	P	O	T	T	E	R	C	C	E	D	T
E	O	O	I	O	X	P	E	I	R	S	E
U	S	N	C	A	C	W	E	A	V	E	R
N	T	I	K	S	V	A	S	N	A	L	E
D	I	S	E	T	B	R	R	T	T	E	S
E	O	T	E	A	T	A	S	T	E	R	T

COOL FACT

Space travellers are known by different names in different countries. Most of the time they are called astronauts. In Russia, they are called cosmonauts, while Chinese space travellers are given the name taikonauts or *yǔ háng yuán*.

Cool Quiz

Did you find any other profession in the maze?

1. A deep sea diver who uses underwater breathing apparatus.

2. A person who is trained to travel into space.

3. A funny person, in a circus, who makes people laugh.

4. A person who entertains an audience with his amazing tricks.

5. A person who makes cloth from thread.

6. A person who uses a wheel or a kiln to make earthenware.

7. A person whose works are displayed in galleries and museums.

8. A person who performs in films or plays.

9. A person who makes interesting, often funny sketches, to tell a story in pictures.

10. A person whose job is to distinguish between different types of teas by tasting them.

MI

Cooking with the Five Senses

A. *Match the dishes with their descriptions. Also write the name of the dish in the space provided.*

1.

____

2.

____

3.

____

4.

____

5.

____

6.

____

a. salty rice dish cooked with vegetables and whole spices

b. salty flatbread, with a filling of mashed vegetables

c. vegetables coated with batter and fried

d. dish of soup-like consistency made of lentils and spices

e. white fluffy and spongy rice cakes eaten with coconut chutney and sambar

f. sweet milky rice pudding seasoned with saffron and dry fruits

B. *Now answer these questions. You can discuss them with your friend.*

1. Name any five vegetables traditionally used in the dishes described above.

   a. _______________
   b. _______________
   c. _______________
   d. _______________
   e. _______________

COOL FACT

Gol gappe, *panipuri* and *puchka* are all names of the same street food in different parts of India.

2. Which is your favourite dish? Describe it in one or two sentences. Also draw or paste its picture.

____

____

____

____

C. *Here's a grid with words related to the sights, sounds, smells, tastes and textures of foods. The words may be used to describe the food while it is being prepared or while it is being eaten.*

Sights	Sounds	Smells	Tastes	Textures
golden	bubbling	sharp	tangy	hot
pink	popping	spicy	crispy	sticky
colourful	crunchy	buttery	spicy	cold
round	slurpy	pungent	salty	gooey
dark	whirring	sugary	sweet	jammy

Choose any three words, from the table above, that you feel would describe the foods given below. Write them against the food. Choose the best descriptive words.

	Word # 1	Word # 2	Word # 3
Candyfloss			
Ice cream			
Popcorn			
Biscuits			
Hot and Sour Soup			
Bhelpuri			

INDIA

5 Let's Go East

Each of these states has three descriptive statements. Identify them and write the correct numbers in the space under the state name.

Bihar	Jharkhand	Odisha	West Bengal

1. It is home to Nalanda, one of the oldest universities of the world.

2. Its name means 'bushland'.

3. Howrah Bridge and the Sunderbans are found in this state.

4. Home to the world famous Olive Ridley Sea Turtles

5. Its name comes from the Sanskrit word for Buddhist monastery.

6. Its capital is Ranchi.

7. It is called *Utkala* in the Indian national anthem.

8. Satyajit Ray, Rabindranath Tagore and Netaji Subhash Chandra Bose are some of its famous personalities.

9. The Madhubani style of painting comes from the town of Madhuban in this state.

10. *Santhal*, *Oraon*, *Munda*, *Bhumij* and *Birhor* are some of the tribal groups found in this state.

11. The capital of this state used to be the capital of India until 1911.

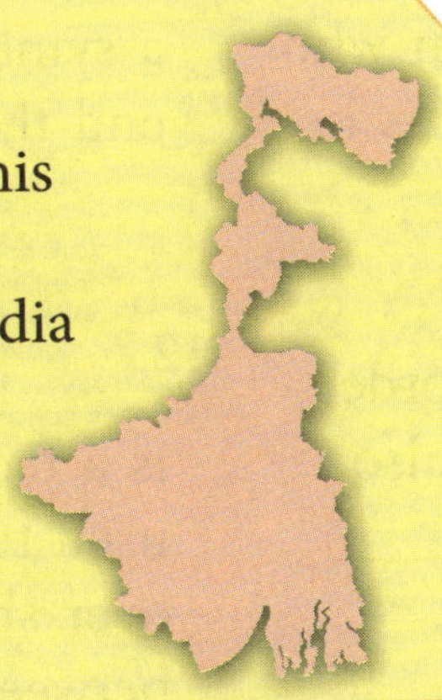

12. Gopalpur-on-Sea and Chandipur are some of its well-known beaches.

COOL FACT

Bengal was a large state until 1947, when it was split into two parts. The eastern part later became an independent country, Bangladesh, while the western part became the Indian state of West Bengal. This explains why an eastern Indian state is called West Bengal.

Colourful Expressions

Colours are often used to express different meanings. Add the word ***black****, white,* *red* *or* *blue* *to complete the sentences below.*

1. The __________ widow is a type of poisonous spider found in North America.

2. The term, __________ elephant, refers to an object whose cost of maintenance is far more than its usefulness.

3. The __________ whale is the largest living animal in the world.

4. Mars is also called the __________ planet.

5. __________ carpet treatment describes the special welcome given to VIP guests.

6. __________ blood is a term used when talking about people who belong to royal families.

7. Appliances, like refrigerators, ovens and mixers, are called __________ goods as they used to have a white enamel finish earlier.

8. The term, __________ sheep, is used to describe a person who is a disgrace to his or her family.

9. In a battle, waving a __________ flag was a symbol of wanting to end the fighting.

10. A special or important day in a person's life is known as a __________ letter day.

11. The flight recorder of an aircraft is also called a __________ box.

12. __________ tooth is a technology that is used to transfer data over short distances between gadgets.

COOL FACT

Did you know that the flight recorder or black box of an aircraft is actually orange in colour? This is to ensure that it can be easily spotted after an aircraft crash.

LANGUAGE AND LITERATURE

7

Words from Shakespeare

A. William Shakespeare, one of the best-known writers in the English language, created more than a thousand new expressions and words.

Solve this crossword to find some of them.

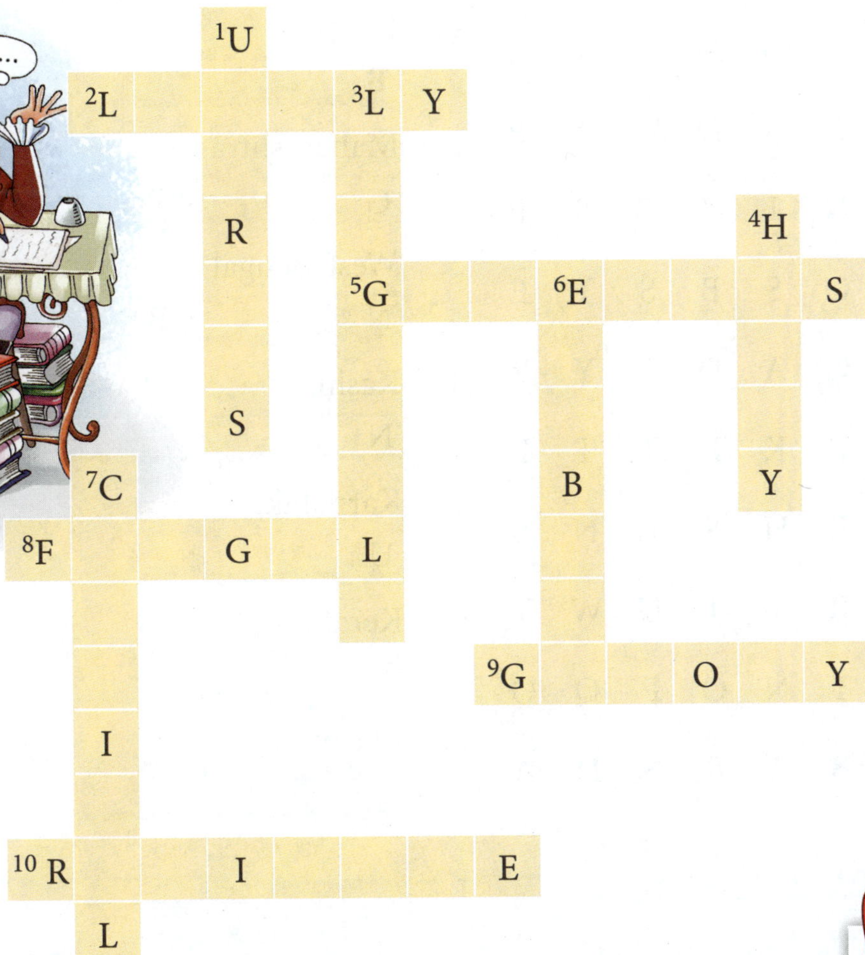

Clues

Across

2. One who has nobody
5. Happy to give things away
8. Plain and costing less
9. Unhappy
10. A kind of glow

Down

1. To take off one's clothes
3. Amusing
4. Rush
6. You see with it
7. Expressing disapproval, careful judgement

B. *Now unscramble these letters to come up with the names of Shakespeare's most famous tragic plays.*

I N G K L R A E

A H T C B E M

M H T L E A

L T O H E L O

COOL FACT

William Shakespeare is believed to have been born on April 23, 1564. He was baptised on April 26 that year. Interestingly, he died on April 23, 1616.

Happy New Year

India has many traditional New Year celebrations, often as harvest festivals or to mark the movement of the Sun or Moon.

A. *Find seven traditional new year names in the word search. The state or region is given as a clue along with the starting letters.*

A	C	E	V	O	B	M	G	T	U
G	U	D	I	P	A	D	W	A	P
A	P	I	S	N	I	Y	E	S	P
G	P	S	H	O	S	B	S	T	E
A	T	T	U	G	A	D	I	Y	R
M	H	R	X	Z	K	E	T	T	E
N	A	V	R	E	H	S	E	N	S
E	P	I	E	R	I	T	U	W	T
O	N	C	S	T	N	O	P	Q	O
N	A	B	A	B	A	R	S	H	A

1. Punjab
   B _ _ _ _ _ _ _
2. Maharashtra
   G _ _ _ P _ _ _ _
3. West Bengal
   N _ _ _ B _ _ _ _ _
4. Kashmir
   N _ _ _ _ _
5. Karnataka
   U _ _ _ _
6. Kerala
   V _ _ _ _
7. Marwar
   T _ _ _ _ _

Cool Activity

Tamizh Puthandu, Sajibu Nongma Panba and Rongali Bihu are also names of New Year celebrations. Find out in which states or regions they are celebrated. Write them here.

1. ____________ 2. ____________ 3. ____________

B. *What is the traditional New Year in your state called? Write it below.*

____

Reading Traffic Signs

A. *Each description given below matches one of the two traffic signs shown. Tick (✓) the sign that matches the description. One has been done for you.*

1. a. b.

slippery road

2. a. b.

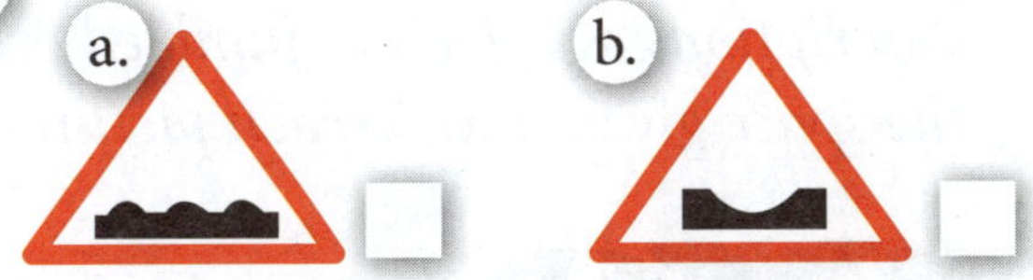

speed breaker ahead

3. a. b.

dual carriageway ends

4. a. b.

level crossing

5. a. b.

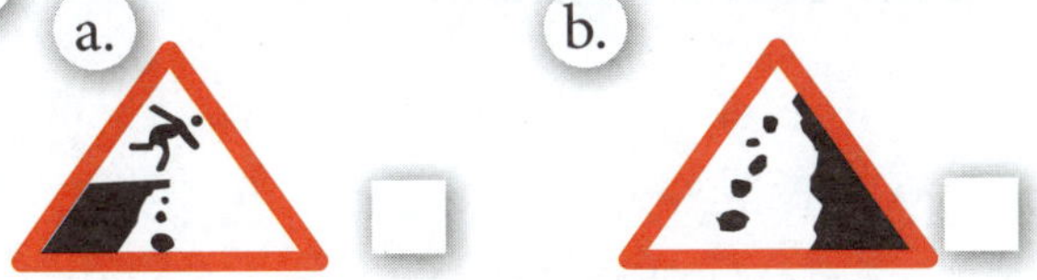

falling rocks

6. a. b.

T-junction

7. a. b.

hairpin bend

8. a. b.

road widens

B. *Do you know any other traffic signs? Where have you seen them? Can you draw a few and also write what they mean?*

8

Chocolate

Which popular product is made from the seeds of the Theobroma cacao plant? Well, the answer is chocolate. Theobroma means 'food of the Gods'. Isn't that an apt name?

A. *Below is the process of making chocolate. The pictures are given in the correct order. The descriptions are given in jumbled order. Write the correct number of the description in the space given next to each picture.*

1. 

2. 

3. 

4. 

5. 

a. After fermentation, the beans are dried in the sun.

b. The beans and pulp are removed from the pods and the beans are allowed to ferment.

c. The dried beans are then cleaned, sorted and roasted.

d. The shells are removed from the roasted beans, to take out the 'nibs' inside.

e. Ripe cacao pods are harvested from the trees.

f. This is then divided into cocoa solids and cocoa butter.

6. 

g. The chocolate liquid is then mixed with cocoa butter in different amounts to make various types of chocolates—dark, milk or white.

7. 

h. The nibs are ground and made into liquid to produce a 'pure chocolate' liquid.

8. 

So, as you see, the 'food for the Gods' goes through a lot before you unwrap that delicious bar or piece of chocolate.

B. *Now rearrange the letters in these jumbled words to come up with the names of some famous brands of chocolates found in India.*

1.	YKLMI ARB	___________	2.	CMNUH	___________
3.	VEIF RSTA	___________	4.	VULEBRILON	___________
5.	RPEK	___________	6.	TKATKI	___________
7.	RIYAD KMIL	___________	8.	LAUM	___________
9.	RAMS	___________	10.	DRINKE OYJ	___________

COOL FACT Cacao beans were used as money by people in Central America. The Aztec Emperor Montezuma was considered very, very rich because apart from all the gold he owned, he also had a store with millions of cacao pods.

9 Hill Stations

We enjoy spending our holidays at hill stations.

Read the clues and unscramble the jumbled letters to form names of hill stations. Then, from the help box, choose and write the state in which each is situated. One has been done for you.

Jumbled name	Correct name	Clue	State name
1. NILATANI	Nainital	The name of this hill station, in the Kumaon Hills, is a combination of the words for eye and lake.	Uttarakhand
2. TOYO		Known as the Queen of the Nilgiris	
3. OMUTN BUA		The only hill station in India's largest state, located in the Aravalli Range	
4. ATMHRAEN		A pedestrian-only hill station in the Sahyadri mountain range	
5. IAMNLA		Further uphill from Kullu, found in the abode of snow	
6. ULGARMG		Found in the Pir Panjal Range of the Himalayas, its name means 'meadow of flowers'.	

Gujarat	Tamil Nadu	Kerala	Maharashtra
Uttarakhand	Himachal Pradesh	Haryana	Rajasthan
Jammu and Kashmir	Karnataka	Madhya Pradesh	West Bengal

Jumbled name	Correct name	Clue	State name
7. APSATAUR		The only hill station in India's westernmost state	
8. MRNOI SHLIL		A hill station in the Shivalik Range, it gives the state its tourism logo—the peafowl	
9. DMAIKREI		Also known as Mercara, found in the southern part of the Western Ghats	
10. UMNARN		Known for its tea plantations, found in the deep south of the Western Ghats	
11. APCMHAHRI		In the heart of India, called the Queen of the Satpuras	
12. ADREEJLNGI		Nestled in the Himalayas, you can see the majestic Kanchenjunga from here	

COOL FACT

Shimla, one of India's best known hill stations, was the summer capital of India from 1864 to 1939 during British rule.

ART

10

Wonders of the Ancient World

The Seven Wonders of the Ancient World are a list of monuments that were compiled by writers as places to be visited and seen. Almost like a modern day guide book.

In this map of the ancient world, you can see pictures of the seven wonders. Fill in the correct letter in the table containing their names and locations.

Name, Location	Letter
1. Great Pyramid of Giza, Egypt	
2. Hanging Gardens of Babylon, Iraq	
3. Temple of Artemis at Ephesus, Turkey	
4. Statue of Zeus at Olympia, Greece	
5. Mausoleum at Halicarnassus, Turkey	
6. Colossus of Rhodes, Greece	
7. Lighthouse of Alexandria, Egypt	

COOL FACT

The Great Pyramid of Giza, the oldest of the Seven Wonders of the Ancient World, is the only one out of the seven ancient wonders to survive today.

11

AROUND THE WORLD

Money Exchange

Each country has its own currency. Sometimes, more than one country uses currency units of the same name. Great Britain and Egypt both use the pound, but they are different currencies.

A. *Put the countries, from the help box, in the correct columns.*

Rupee	Dollar	Dinar

Canada
Sri Lanka
Mauritius
New Zealand
Australia
Hong Kong
Libya
Algeria
Nepal
Maldives
USA
Pakistan
Kuwait
Iraq
Jordan

B. *Match these countries with their currencies.*

a.

Real

1. China
2. Brazil
3. South Africa
4. Russia
5. Malaysia

b.

Yuan

c.

Rouble

d.

Rand

e.

Ringgit

COOL FACT The Euro is the currency unit used in most countries of the European Union. Find out which countries use the Euro.

Countries Linked to Words

Many expressions in English are made up of combinations of country names and common words thanks to historical or cultural association of some things with particular countries..

A. *Choose the names of countries from the box and complete the expressions. The country flags are clues.*

Danish	French	Portuguese	Turkish	Swiss	Russian
German	Indian	Japanese	Arabian	Chinese	Persian

1. 
______________ ink

2. 
__________ man-o'-war

3. 
______________ towel

4. 
______________ fries

5. 
______________ salad

6. 
____________ checkers

7. 
______________ knife

8. 
______________ fan

9. 
______________ mare

10. 
____________ shepherd

11. 
______________ carpet

12. 
______________ pastry

COOL FACT

In a stadium, groups of spectators often briefly stand, yell and raise their arms. The combined movement of these groups one after the other looks like a wave. During the 1986 FIFA World Cup, this was first seen in Mexico, which is why it is called a Mexican Wave.

B. *Now match the country-name-expressions with their pictures from the jumbled set given. One has been done for you.*

a.

11

b.

c.

d.

e.

f.

g.

h.

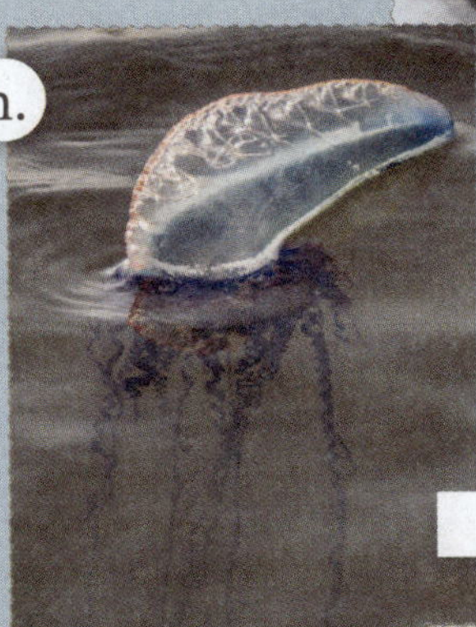

i.

j.

k.

l.

Dramatic Nature!

A. The natural world is an exciting stage for some spectacular events. Some are disasters, while others are simply surprising.

Complete this open crossword about disasters using the clues.

Clues

Across

1. This word comes from the Roman god of fire. Hawaii, Iceland and Mount Fujiyama in Japan are examples of this occurrence.
3. Japan is a country in which this disaster is very common. So, many buildings in Japan are built in such a manner that they would not collapse when it occurs.

4. This natural disaster occurs in the ocean. It is characterised by strong winds, in the centre of which is a clear, calm region called the eye.
6. This is a rapid spinning tube of air sometimes called a twister. It is composed of the fastest winds on Earth, taking many shapes and sizes.
8. This is a kind of strong storm which most often forms in the northwest Pacific Ocean. Its name has been derived from a Chinese word which means 'great wind'.

Down

2. This common occurrence appears as a bright flash in the sky. It is usually followed by a clap or rumble of thunder.
5. This calamity is a result of very little water in the atmosphere, causing little or no rain. If it lasts for a long time, it can cause famine or severe food shortage.
6. The name of this huge wave wall comes from the Japanese word meaning 'harbour wave'. In December 2004, this disastrous wave uncovered the lost city of Mahabalipuram in the Indian Ocean.
7. An overflow of water from rivers, lakes or excess rain can result in this condition. To stay safe during this calamity, one should go to the highest ground or floor possible.

B. *Natural disasters are measured by using special instruments or scales. Match these common scales with the phenomena that they are used to measure.*

1.	Deep Ocean Assessment and Reporting (DART)	a.	Earthquake intensity
2.	Beaufort Scale	b.	Tsunami
3.	Richter Scale	c.	Tropical cyclone's speed of wind

COOL FACT The names of some cyclones that occur in the Indian Ocean are *Agni*, *Akash*, *Bijli*, *Jal*, *Lehar*, *Megh*, *Sagar* and *Vayu*. Even you can suggest a name for a cyclone to the Indian Meteorological Department.

INDIA

15 Indian Brides and Grooms

Indian weddings are known for their variety, colours and festivity. Here are names of some brides, regions and grooms with few clues.

Match the brides with their regions/states and their grooms.

Brides

1.

crown made of white *pith*

2.

white gown and veil

3.

silk *saree*, flowers in hair

4.

saree with pleats at the back, brooch

Coorg (Karnataka)	Bengal	Goa (Catholic)	Tamil Nadu

Grooms

a.

white tunic, silk belt, stitched turban

b.

starched *dhoti* with a distinct fan pattern

c.

bare-chested, *dhoti* with 'peacock-eye' border

d.

formal suit

Brides

5.

green bangles, *nath* or nose ring, veil made of flowers and pearls

6.

thick, wool or velvet robe called *goncha*, headpiece with turquoise stones

7.

gold *kalire* dangling from wrists, red and white bangles

8.

lehenga and veil, nose ring, *sindoor* in hair

Uttar Pradesh   Ladakh (J&K)   Punjab (Sikh)   Maharashtra

Grooms

e.

turban, decorated sword

f.

special turban, veil made of flowers and pearls

g.

robe called *goncha*, embroidered waistcoat, boots, cap

h.

floral or pearl veil called *sehra* covering the face

COOL FACT

In ancient times, women from Indian royal families could choose a bridegroom out of a group of assembled suitors. This event was called a *swayamvar*.

SCIENCE

16 Manufacturing Fruit Juice

Here are some pictures and statements about the process of making fruit juice in a factory. They are not in the correct sequence. Put them in the correct order.

1.

First, fruit is harvested.

Finally, the juice is cooled and the bottles labelled and stored.

2.

The next step is to cut, slice or core it.

3.

Pasteurization, that is, heating at 80-90ºC for 15 minutes is done at this stage.

4.

5.

Bottles and caps are boiled for at least 10 minutes to sterilize them.

The bottles are filled and the caps sealed.

The fruit is turned into pulp.

The fruit is sorted and graded.

Then, it is washed.

The pulp is filtered.

COOL FACT

The popular Indian cool drink, *Rooh Afza,* was created from herbs and pure fruit and vegetable juices by Hakeem Hafiz Abdul Majeed, the founder of the Jamia Hamdard University, in 1907.

17

Let's Visit the UK

Capital: London
Currency: British Pound
Flag: Union Jack

The Head of State of the United Kingdom is a King or a Queen, known as a monarch. Who is the current monarch of the UK? ____________________

A. *Match the inventions with their British inventors.*

Inventions	Inventors
1. TV	a. Tim Berners-Lee
2. Steam engine	b. James Hargreaves
3. Steam locomotive/train	c. James Watt
4. Spinning jenny	d. George Stephenson
5. World Wide Web	e. John Logie Baird

B. *Here are the names and pictures of six English authors with some of their most famous characters. Match them.*

1.

Enid Blyton

2.

Arthur Conan Doyle

3.

William Shakespeare

4.

Charles Dickens

5.

Agatha Christie

6.

JK Rowling

a. Sherlock Holmes
b. Hercule Poirot
c. Noddy
d. Harry Potter
e. Hamlet
f. Oliver Twist

C. *London is an exciting city and has many well-known landmarks. Connect the clues, the pictures and the names.*

1. Ding dong bell!
2. Opens up for ships to pass
3. The home of cricket
4. A grass court
5. Platform nine and three-quarters
6. Splits London into two
7. London underground
8. The Queen's home
9. Sherlock Holmes lived here
10. The original waxworks museum

a.

b.

c.

d.

e.

f.
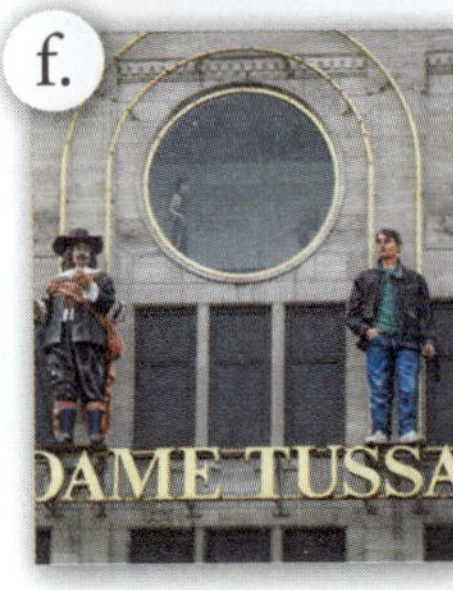

g.

h.

i.

j.

i. Baker Street

ii. The Thames

iii. Big Ben

iv. Madame Tussaud's

v. The Tube

vi. Lord's Cricket Ground

vii. Wimbledon

viii. King's Cross Station

ix. Buckingham Palace

x. Tower Bridge

COOL FACT The United Kingdom of Great Britain and Northern Ireland consists of Great Britain, made up of England, Scotland and Wales and Northern Ireland, which is the northern part of the neighbouring island called Ireland.

Game of the World

Play this game and check out your knowledge of the world!

Start at Square **a**, *answer the question and then follow the instructions. Each player will move through the game with a coloured token. The player who reaches FINISH! first, wins.*

c

Fill in the blank. The ______ joins North America with South America.

i. Suez Canal → b

ii. Isthmus of Panama → r

d

The Cape of Good Hope is at the southern tip of

i. South America. → m

ii. Africa. → w

e

Which is the smallest continent in the world?

i. Australia → r

ii. Antarctica → m

b

The Palk Strait separates

i. India and Sri Lanka. → u

ii. India and Bangladesh. → j

f

The smallest ocean in the world is the Indian Ocean.

i. True → e

ii. False → v

a

India is surrounded by three water bodies, Bay of Bengal, Indian Ocean and

i. Mediterranean Sea. → q

ii. Arabian Sea. → t

g

GOAL!

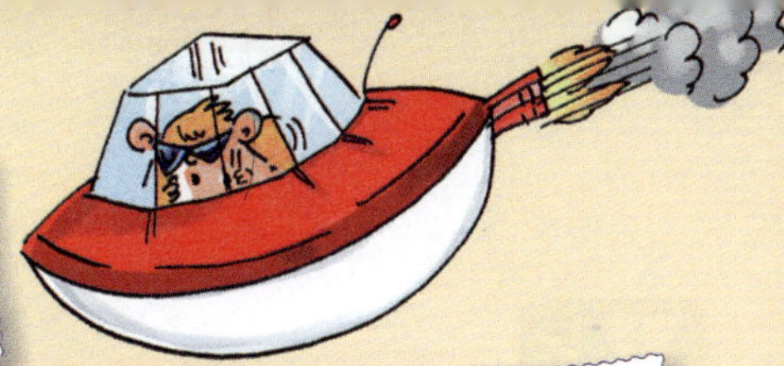

n

Kalahari, Gobi and Atacama are names of

i. lakes. → b

ii. deserts. → u

q

Puerto Rico, Java and Mariana are all names of

i. volcanic islands. → y

ii. ocean trenches. → d

r

The Jura, Pyrenees and Dolomites are all mountain ranges in

i. Africa. → h

ii. Europe. → u

m

Which of these statements about the world's tallest peak, Mount Everest, is true?

i. It is slowly sinking. → h

ii. It is slowly rising. → r

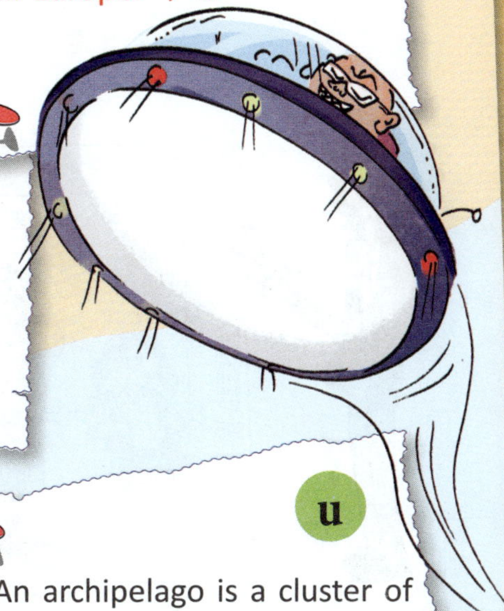

s

The spectacular Grand Canyon is in

i. USA. → k

ii. Mexico. → v

k

A peninsula is

i. a water body surrounded by landmasses on three sides. → c

ii. a landmass surrounded by water bodies on three sides. → e

t

India falls completely in the Northern Hemisphere.

i. True → f

ii. False → s

u

An archipelago is a cluster of islands. Which is the biggest archipelago in the world?

i. Japan → j

ii. Indonesia → g

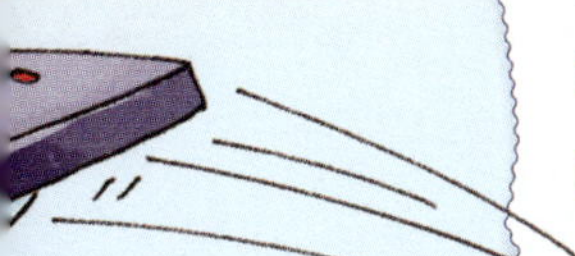

j

Under which ocean is the longest mountain range in the world?

i. Atlantic → g

ii. Pacific → c

y

Which of these mountain ranges would you find in Africa?

i. Atlas → e

ii. Andes → m

v

Aurora Australis is also known as

i. The Northern Lights. → c

ii. The Southern Lights. → r

h

Which country does Greenland belong to?

i. Denmark → n

ii. Iceland → c

w

Lakshadweep is a cluster of

i. volcanic islands. → h

ii. coral islands. → n

Behaviour in Public Places

Knowledge is important, but there is no substitute for good manners and etiquette.

Read the following statements about behaviour in public places. Mark examples of good manners with a ☺ and bad manners with a ☹.

1. If a stranger wishes you good morning in a lift, it is better to stay quiet than to respond.

2. If you want to listen to music in a public place, use the headphones so as not to disturb others.

3. While at a cinema hall, you can talk softly to your friend on a mobile phone.

4. As soon as an aeroplane lands, you should stay seated with your seatbelt fastened until the "fasten seatbelt" sign is switched off.

5. If you have an upper berth in a train, you can sit on your berth and dangle your feet.

6. You should quickly walk upstairs or downstairs while on an escalator, so you will reach even faster.

7. People inside a lift should be allowed to exit before people outside step in.

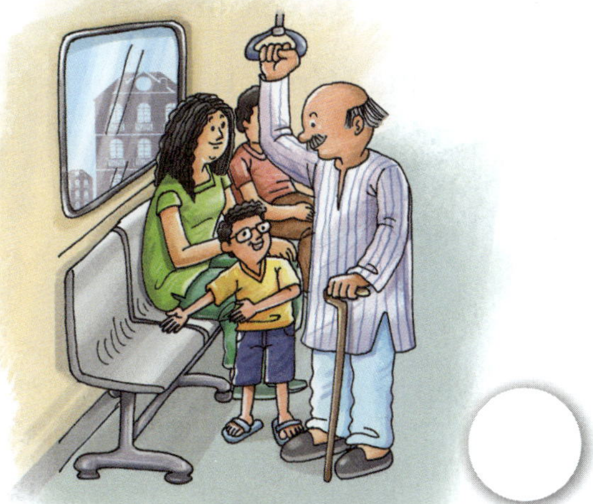

8. In a bus or metro, it is good manners to offer your seat to senior citizens.

9. It is good practice to greet and thank security staff who frisk you or check your bags at malls, airports and other public places.

10. When using a lift, if you are on the 4th floor and you want to go to the ground floor, you should press the UP button so that the lift comes up.

Types of Doctors

When we are unwell, we rush to a doctor. The first doctor we meet is usually the GP or General Practitioner. But many doctors do extra studies and specialise in treating diseases or illnesses related to specific parts of the body. Their names are usually taken from Greek or Latin. Read this list of Greek and Latin words (some are part-words) with their meanings in English.

Greek or Latin	English
Kardia (Greek)	Heart
Dens, dentis (Latin)	Tooth
Derma, dermat (Greek)	Skin
Gyne (Greek)	Woman
Neuron (Greek)	Tendon, sinew, nerve
Oncos (Greek)	Tumour, volume
Orthos (Greek)	Straight, correct, normal
Pes/Ped (Latin)	Foot
Paedos (Greek)	Child
Psyche (Greek)	Breath, life, soul
Iatros/-iatry/-iatrist, -iatrician	Healer/field/doctor specialising in medicine of a certain body component/branch
Plastos (Greek)	Surgical repair, reconstruction

COOL FACT

The basic educational degree needed to become a doctor is MBBS, which stands for **Bachelor of Medicine, Bachelor of Surgery**, which should be MBMS, but the term is taken from the Latin *Medicinae Baccalaureus, Baccalaureus Chirurgiae*.

Now complete the definitions. Match the specialists with their area of specialisation.

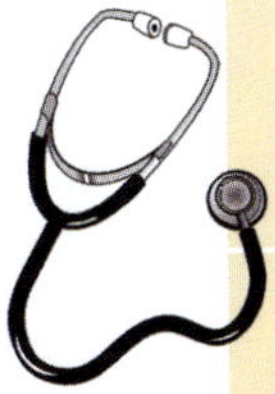

1. A Cardiologist
2. A Dentist
3. A Gynaecologist
4. A Dermatologist
5. A Neurologist
6. An Oncologist
7. An ENT specialist
8. A Paediatrician
9. An Orthopedic Surgeon
10. A Plastic Surgeon
11. Psychiatrist
12. Surgeon

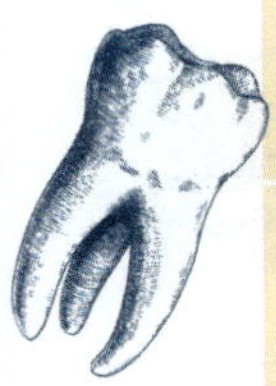

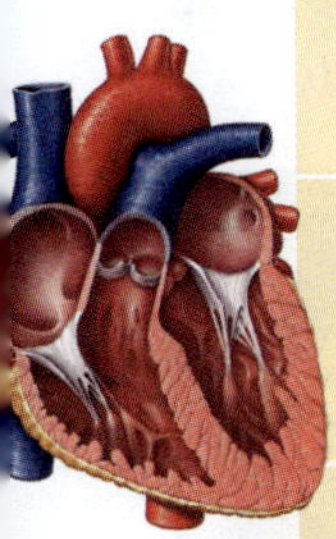

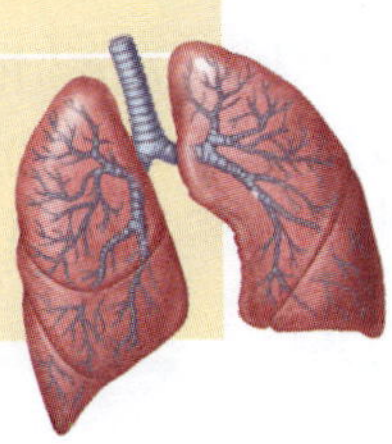

a. Is an expert on the human brain and nervous system, and illnesses related to these

b. Is a doctor who specialises in treating patients with mental illness and behavioural disorders

c. Is a doctor who specialises in ailments related to the ear, nose and throat.

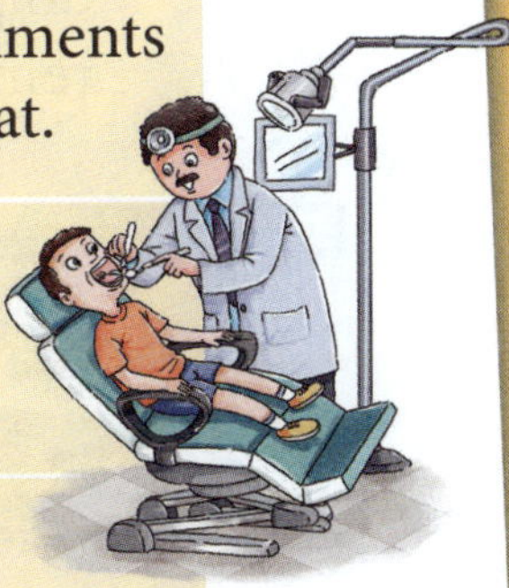

d. Works with the human mouth, teeth and gums, and treats ailments related to them.

e. Performs a wide variety of operations from the head to the feet

f. Treats problems related to the skeletal system, such as broken bones

g. Is an expert at treating the heart and the many diseases and issues related to it.

h. Is a doctor who studies the skin, and diseases related to it

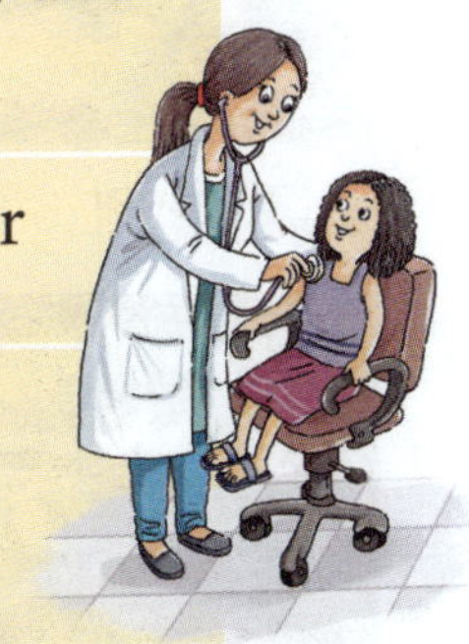

i. Helps to treat and prevent cancer

j. Works with infants, children and adolescents on a variety of health isssues.

k. Specialises in dealing with women, childbirth and related issues

l. Is a doctor who performs cosmetic surgery that can change the way a person looks

12

Animals Adapt

All animals adapt to their habitat. Use the clues in the sentences to fill in the blanks. Choose the answers from the help box.

dolphin	penguin	seal	hippopotamus
reindeer	starfish	jellyfish	octopus

dolphin

penguin

seal

octopus

1. The many-legged __________ does not have a skeleton. So it can squeeze through tiny cracks between undersea rocks.
2. A __________ lives on land, in water and on ice. It has flippers that help it to swim in water.
3. A __________ moves about with the help of a number of transparent tube like hairs called tentacles.
4. The __________ is huge, but a thick layer of fat under its skin helps it to keep its head above water and float.
5. The __________ has wide hooves that prevent it from sinking in the snow.
6. The __________ breathes through a hole called a blow hole on top of its head.
7. The __________, which looks like it is wearing a black and white coat, has feet that do not freeze because they are covered with feathers and body fat.
8. The __________, also called a sea star, has no brains and no blood. Its nervous system is spread through its arms and its blood is actually filtered sea water.

hippopotamus

jellyfish

starfish

reindeer

COOL FACT

The Basilisk Lizard, found in Central and South America, has flaps between its toes that allow it to run short distances on water surfaces. It actually looks like it is running on water!

The Number 5

A. *Connect the three columns to come up with five sets of five:*

1. The Kada, Kirpan, Kesh, Kanghi and Kachcha are the	a. Five rivers	i. Created by Enid Blyton
2. The Shahada, Salat, Zakat, Sawm and Haj are the...	b. Five rings	ii. on the Olympic Flag
3. The Jhelum, Chenab, Ravi, Sutlej and Beas are the	c. Five 'k's	iii. of Islam
4. Julian, Dick, Anne and George (Georgina)– and Timothy the dog are together known as the	d. Five Pillars	iv. of Punjab
5. Europe, Asia, Africa, Australia and the Americas are represented by the	e. Famous Five	v. of Sikhism

B. *The word 'panch' means 5; and is a root word of several terms that are commonly known to Indians.*

Complete the following words beginning with 'panch' using the answers given in the help box. But watch out! There are two extra answers.

PANCH ________	A mixture of 5 foods used in worship, normally honey, liquid jaggery, milk, yoghurt and ghee
PANCH ________	A traditional calendar used in India for astrological purposes as well
PANCH ________	A collection of fables divided into 5 parts written by Vishnu Sharma
PANCH ________	5 principles of peaceful coexistence, the basis of India's foreign policy
PANCH ________	A system of government in villages where a set of 5 persons would settle disputes

panch-phoron	panchang	panchamrit	panchatantra
panchashila	panch-pakhdi	panchayat	

INDIA

19

Nature's Bounty in North East India

The North East Region has some unique, unusual and matchless examples of natural beauty and features.

Read these sentences about the region and fill in the blanks with the names of the states themselves, rivers, lakes, mountains and other features.

1. The Tsangpo river enters ______________ from Tibet and is then known as the Siang. When it flows into Assam, this mighty river is called the ______________.
2. Loktak Lake near Moirang in Manipur is the largest freshwater lake in Northeast India. It is famous for the *phumdis* (mix of vegetation, soil, and organic matter at various stages of decomposition) on its surface. Also floating on the lake is ______________, the only floating national park in the world.
3. Umiam Lake (commonly known as Barapani Lake) is a reservoir located in the hills 15 km to the north of Shillong in ______________ It was created by damming the Umiam river in the early 1960s.
4. According to the India State of Forest Report (ISFR)of 2015, ______________, sometimes called the 'peninsula state' because it is surrounded by foreign countries on 3 sides, has 88.93 percentage of forest cover, the highest forest cover in percentage terms among all states in India
5. Nagaland's highest mountain is ______________, which, at a height of 3826 m and a prominence of 2885 m, soars above the surrounding peaks at the mountainous border of Nagaland and Myanmar.
6. Almost the entire state of Sikkim is hilly, with an elevation ranging from 280 metres (920 ft) to 8,586 metres (28,169 ft). The summit of ______________., the world's third-highest peak, is the state's highest point, situated on the border between Sikkim and Nepal.
7. Tiny ______________ , the third smallest state of India after Goa and Sikkim, has five ranges of Boromura, Atharamura, Longtharai, Shakhan and Jampui Hills that run north to south.

COOL FACT

The North East receives more than 10,000 mm of rainfall every year. Cherrapunji and nearby Mawnsynram in Meghalaya are the wettest places in India, and perhaps the earth!

Mount Saramati | Tripura | Keibul Lamjao | Mount Kanchenjunga
Meghalaya | Arunachal Pradesh | Brahmaputra | Mizoram

Internet Country Codes

All official websites in India have the country domain name .in. Other well-known country specific domain names are .us, .uk, etc.

A. *Identify and write the country names from these easy domain names.*

1. .cn ______________________
2. .jp ______________________
3. .fr ______________________
4. .it ______________________
5. .ru ______________________
6. .br ______________________
7. .ca ______________________
8. .au ______________________
9. .nz ______________________
10. .pk ______________________

B. *Some internet country codes are used for business, personal and other reasons because of their unique names. Match these cool codes with the countries. But watch out! There are four answers that do not match with any domain name.*

Djibouti	Mauritius	Dominica	Tuvalu
Turkey	Montenegro	Federated States of Micronesia	
Macedonia	Denmark	Democratic Republic of the Congo	

1. .cd __________ 2. .tv __________ 3. .fm __________

4. .dj __________ 5. .me __________ 6. .mu __________

COOL FACT

Some common countries have domain names that look difficult, but simply match their names in the local language. These include .de for Germany (Deutschland), .ch for Switzerland (Confoederatio Helvetica), .es for Spain (España), .za for South Africa (Zuid Afrika) and .is for Iceland (Island).

PIN Codes

When you write an address in India, you would realize it normally ends with a six-digit number. This is the ***P**ostal* ***I**ndex* ***N**umber* or PIN Code. The PIN code on a letter or package helps a postman to deliver letters to the correct place in India.

A. *Let us understand what these numbers mean, by taking a real example, 211001.*

The **first** number tells us which of India's 9 postal regions this letter is addressed to.

The **second** number indicates the sub-region. It is normally read together with the first number.

The **third** number indicates the sorting district within the region.

The **fourth** number indicates the 'route' on which the destination post office is located. It is normally read together with the fifth and the sixth numbers.

The **fifth** and the **sixth** numbers tell us which specific post office the letter has to be delivered to.

2	1	1	0	0	1

In this case it is '2' which stands for Uttar Pradesh and Uttarakhand.

Here it is '1' which together with the first digit stands for '21', that is, the sub-region in which Allahabad falls.

Allahabad GPO is in Sorting District 1.

Here the last three digits make '001' which stands for the Allahabad General Post Office or GPO.

B. *Given below are some addresses. Write the correct pin codes to these addresses from the choices given in the help box. Use the PIN code zones map of India for help. But watch out! There are four extra options that do not match any address.*

731204	171001
517352	221001
110011	571352
450001	400001
362268	600015

COOL FACT

The Supreme Court of India was the first institution in India to be given an exclusive PIN code—110201 as the court gets a lot of letters every day.

1. The Principal, Rishi Valley School, Madanapalle, Andhra Pradesh ____________

2. Upacharya or Vice Chancellor, Visva Bharati University, Santiniketan, West Bengal ______________

3. The Chief Executive Officer, Tata Steel Limited, Bombay House, 3rd Floor, 24 Homi Mody Street, Fort, Mumbai, Maharashtra ______________

4. The Postmaster, Shimla G.P.O., Shimla, Himachal Pradesh ______________

5. The Prime Minister of India, 5 Race Course Road, New Delhi ____________

6. Somnath Temple, Shree Somnath Trust, Prabhas Patan, Ta. Veraval, District Girsomnath, Gujarat ____________

20

Extinct Animals

The International Union for Conservation of Nature (IUCN) regularly publishes the Red List of Threatened Species, which provides information on the conservation status and distribution of plants, fungi and animals.

IUCN has divided the levels of conservation of animals into seven major categories as follows.

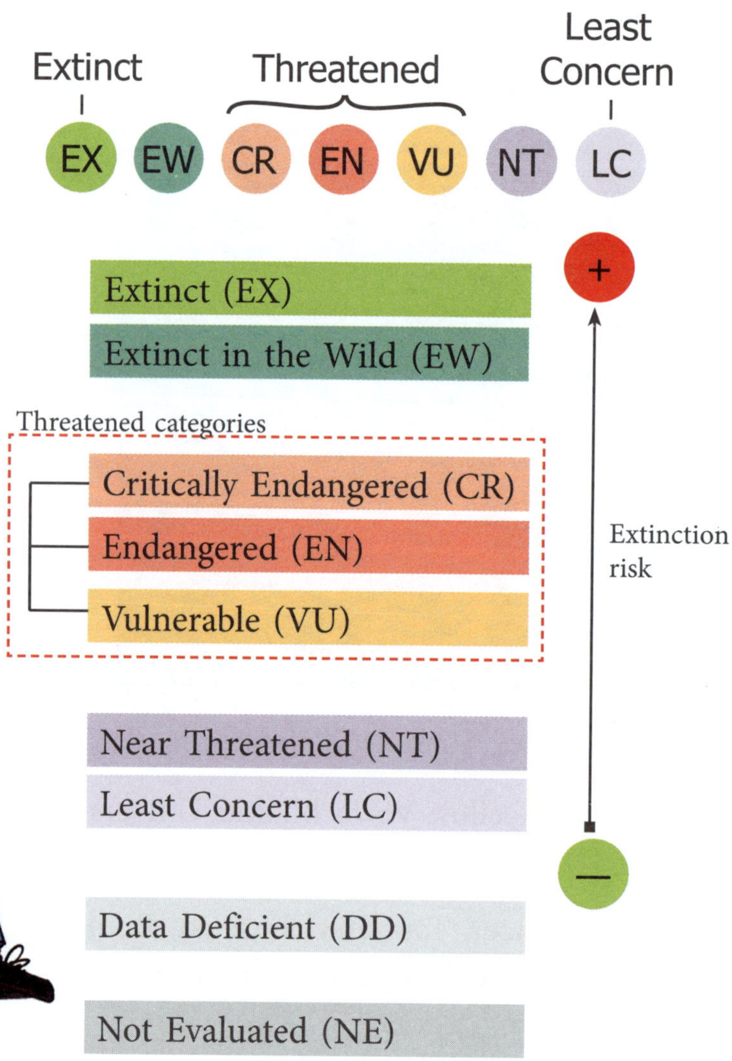

COOL FACT The Quagga, an extinct animal, was named after the warning call made by the zebra in the plains, which sounded like 'kwa-ha-ha'.

Here is a list of animals that became extinct due to cruel human activities, like hunting. Match these six animals with their pictures and descriptive statements.

Name	Picture	Description
1. The Great Auk	a. 	i. Extinct since the early 1970s, it was found in forests, near water, throughout central Russia, Afghanistan, Turkey, Iran and Mongolia. It is also known as the Hyrcanian Tiger or the Turan Tiger.
2. Quagga	b. 	ii. Large carnivorous marsupial, native to continental Australia, Tasmania and New Guinea, extinct since 1936
3. Dodo	c. 	iii. Looked like a cross between a horse and a zebra, this animal lived in South Africa until the late 19th century.
4. Caspian Tiger	d. 	iv. Once the most abundant birds in North America, scientists are trying to bring back these birds by using the DNA of its closest relative, the band-tailed pigeon.
5. Passenger Pigeon	e. 	v. Flightless birds who couldn't run, once found on the shores and islands of Northern Europe and North America.
6. Thylacine/ Tasmanian Tiger	f. 	vi. Flightless birds found on the Mauritius Island in the Indian Ocean, they were hunted to extinction by sailors, for food.

AROUND THE WORLD

21 Sobriquets for Countries

A sobriquet (sob-ri-kay) is a nickname describing a person or place by a feature related to them.

Guess the sobriquet of the following countries from the picture clues and write it in the space provided.

1. Japan is known as the Land of the ______________________.
2. Switzerland is known as the ______________________ of Europe.

3. Cuba is known as the ______________________ of the World.
4. Netherlands is known as the Land of ______________________.

5. Bhutan is known as the Land of ______________________.
6. Thailand is known as the Land of the ______________________.

7. Canada is known as the Land of the ______________________.
8. South Africa is known as the ______________________ Nation.

9. Egypt is known as the ______________________ of the Nile.
10. New Zealand is known as the Land of the ______________________.

COOL FACT Italians call their country *Lo Stivale*, which means 'the boot' because of its shape.

AROUND THE WORLD

22

Let's Visit Brazil

Brazil was the host country of the 2016 Olympic Games.

Currency: Real
Capital: Brasilia
Official Language: Brazilian Portuguese

COOL FACT

There are twenty-seven white stars on the Brazilian flag. They represent the country's twenty-six states and the Federal District.

Fill in the blanks using the words given in the help box.

1. Brazil is the ___________ largest country in the world and the largest country in ___________ America. It shares land borders with all countries on the continent except Ecuador and ___________.
2. The largest city in Brazil is ___________. Another beautiful city is Rio de Janeiro, known for its Copacabana ___________, the iconic statue of ___________ the Redeemer, as well as the ___________ Mountain.
3. The ___________, the biggest river in the world, flows through the world's largest ___________, a teeming jungle that houses twenty percent of the world's bird species, millions of plants, insects and fish, including the deadly ___________.
4. Rio de Janeiro is also known for the ___________, a festival that is celebrated annually before Easter.
5. Brazil is the world's largest producer of ___________.
6. The favourite sport of Brazil is ___________ and one of the best-known Brazilian players is Edson Arantes do Nascimento, also known as ___________.
7. Brazil's unique culture is known for several dance forms including the samba and the ___________.

Christ
South
Chile
lambada
fifth
Sao Paulo
Beach
football
Pele
Sugar Loaf
rainforest
piranha
Amazon
carnival
coffee

NATURAL WORLD

23

Man's Best Friend

Name the dog breeds using these pictures and descriptions as clues.

1.

Named after a place in Canada, these dogs are also used to detect bombs or drugs.

____

2.

A national breed of France, it gets its name from a German word meaning 'to splash about'.

____

3.

Originally from China, they are very friendly and loving dogs. Often called shadow dogs because of their tendency to follow their owners like faithful shadows.

____

4.

Originated in Scotland, they are used as guide dogs for the blind. Also famous as members of detection and rescue teams.

____

Poodle	Labrador	Dalmatian	Golden Retriever
Pug	St. Bernard	Pomeranian	German Shepherd

5.

Originally from Germany, these toy dogs are also called poms or pompoms.

____

6.

Excellent guard dogs, they are named after a part of Croatia. Hugely popular since the film adaptation of a novel by Dodie Smith, '*A Hundred and One* ________.'

____

7.

One of the most intelligent dog breeds, this large dog, sometimes called Alsatian, was originally used to tend sheep in Germany, from where it got its name.

____

8.

A dog that rescues travellers lost in the snow. Nana, the lovable 'governess' of Wendy, John and Michael Darling in *Peter Pan,* belongs to this breed.

____

COOL FACT

Named after a state in Mexico, the Chihuahua is the tiniest dog breed. At the opposite end is the Great Dane, which is so huge that it can comfortably reach the shoulder of an average human adult.

Different Kinds of Waste

Different kinds of waste need to be thrown into different bins. Some kinds can be recycled, others can be used to create soil for growing plants. Electronic waste contains poisonous chemicals and must be handled with great care.

A. *Sort these different kinds of waste into the three bins by writing the letters of the types of waste along the bins.*

1. 

2. 

3. 

a. newspapers
b. mobile phone
c. clothes
d. waste food
e. computer parts
f. vegetable stalks and skins
g. polythene covers
h. batteries
i. nut shells
j. old shoes
k. glass
l. compact discs
m. dry leaves
n. fruit peels
o. bulbs
p. broken toys
q. iron nails
r. mobile chargers
s. egg shells
t. tea leaves
u. phones

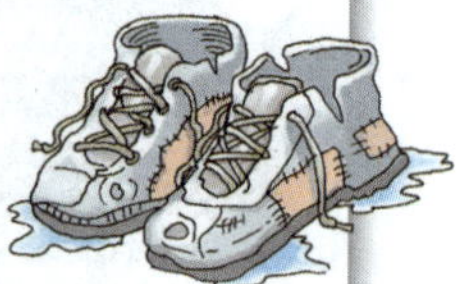

B. *What can we do to reduce waste or dispose it properly in our daily lives? Here are some activities. Mark with a ☺ smiley what you, as a child, can do.*

1. I can dig compost pits and make organic manure by using vegetable and garden wastes.

2. I can set up a small factory to make useful products out of waste material like jute, cotton, paper, etc.

3. I can build bio-gas plants, by using bio-waste such as dung, field or agro-waste to generate fuel.

4. I can build toilets for the poor for proper disposal of human waste.

5. I can give toys, books, colours and pencils to the poorer children in my neighbourhood.

6. I can shop for clothes, shoes or bags less frequently.

7. I can form a team and pick up wrappers, plastic bags, papers, etc., lying around in my neighbourhood, school or playground once a week.

8. I can throw waste into a dustbin.

COOL FACT

In some cities, there are different coloured public bins, green for wet waste (kitchen waste), blue for dry recyclable waste (paper, cardboard, juice cartons, bottles and cans) and red for reject waste (diapers and bandages).

HISTORY

24 How Did Humans Fly?

These pictures and text narrate the story of flying by human beings. Look at them carefully.

1. The Flying Greek—Icarus

2. The Dragon Flies!

3. Leonardo da Vinci

4. The Montgolfier Hot Air Balloon

COOL FACT The first person to fly faster than the speed of sound was an American pilot named Charles 'Chuck' Yeager.

5. Henrich Focke's Helicopter

6. The Jet Engine

7. George Cayley's Glider

8. The Wright Brothers: Inventors of Modern Flight

Read these statements. Mark them T for True and F for False based on the text and pictures given above.

1. Hot-air balloons carried human beings up into the sky, before aeroplanes were invented. ☐
2. George Cayley flew in the first glider he invented. ☐
3. The flying machine invented by Leonardo Da Vinci is called the Ornithopter. ☐
4. The Wright brothers (Wilbur and Orville) flew the first stable flight called Flyer 1. ☐
5. Frank Whittle started an airline called Jet. ☐

INDIA

25 Puppets

India has a long tradition of street theatre, and puppets are a big favourite. These are some traditional puppets from different states of India. They are divided into four types—glove, string, rod and shadow.

A. *Read the names, see the pictures and see where they come from.*

1. Pavakoothu

Glove puppet from Kerala

2. Gombeyatta

String puppet from Karnataka

3. Putul Nautch

Rod puppet from West Bengal

4. Tholu Bommalata

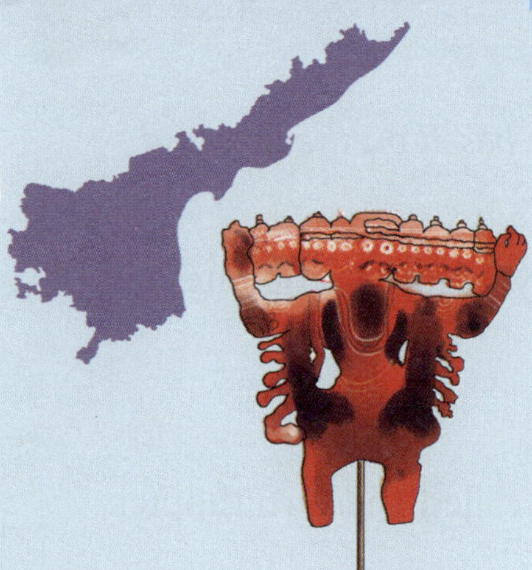

Shadow puppet from Andhra Pradesh

5. Kathikundhei Nach

Glove puppet from Odisha

6. Kathputli

String puppet from Rajasthan

7. Kundhei

String puppet from Odisha

8. Bommalattam

String puppet from Tamil Nadu

9. Kalasutri-bahulye

String puppet from Maharashtra

B. *Do you like puppets? What do you like about them? Tick the boxes next to each statement that you agree with. Tick only the four that you like best.*

1. I like the multicoloured clothes that puppets wear. ☐
2. I like the jerky dance movements of puppets. ☐
3. I like the songs and sounds that puppeteers make while doing a puppet show. ☐
4. I like animal puppets the best. ☐
5. I like the stories that puppeteers tell while making their puppets move. ☐
6. I like to make puppets. ☐
7. I like to pretend to be a puppet or a puppeteer. ☐
8. I like to play 'puppet-puppet' with my friends. ☐
9. I would like to do a puppet show in school. ☐
10. I can make wonderful shadow puppets. ☐

26

All Time Greats in Sports

While we all have our favourite sport stars, there are some who are so much better than others that they can be classified as 'all time greats'.

Link these sports personalities to the sport in which they have achieved world fame and one of their greatest feats.

Sportsperson	Sport	Feat
1.  Don Bradman	a. Golf	i. Three times World Heavyweight Boxing Champion
2.  Tiger Woods	b. Boxing	ii. Won 22 Olympic medals including 18 golds, more than any other sportsperson ever
3.  Mohammad Ali	c. Cricket	iii. Romanian woman who was the first to record a score of perfect ten in gymnastics at the Olympics
4.  Michael Phelps	d. Gymnastics	iv. US golfing sensation—youngest to achieve the career Grand Slam in golf
5.  Nadia Comaneci	e. Swimming	v. Australian batsman with a batting average of 99.94 in test match cricket, the highest ever

6.  Michael Jordan	f. Athletics	vi. Brazilian footballer who scored 1281 career goals, an all-time record
7.  Pele	g. Tennis	vii. The greatest basketball player of all time according to the National Basketball Association of USA
8.  Jesse Owens	h. Hockey	viii. Indian Army officer known as The Wizard, he was part of three Olympic gold-winning teams
9.  Dhyan Chand	i. Basketball	ix. Czech-American woman tennis star who won 167 Singles Titles, the most ever by one player
10.  Martina Navratilova	j. Football	x. US Athlete who won 4 gold medals at the 1936 Olympics, and once broke three world records in 1935

COOL FACT

Do you know which Indian batsman has scored a hundred international centuries? Yes, it is Sachin Tendulkar, who was awarded the Bharat Ratna—India's highest civilian award.

ART

27 

Indian Paintings

Our country India is known for its different forms, styles and schools of painting. Read the clues to answer these questions on the paintings. Words are given in the help box.

1. The oldest form of art in India is a number of paintings that can be seen in ☐☐☐☐☐ especially those at Bhimbetka. Very often, these were painted with a reddish material called Geru, which is still used to paint pottery today.

2. These beautiful paintings are examples of Buddhist art and can be seen at the ☐☐☐☐☐☐ Caves in Maharashtra.

3. The Mughal Emperors, especially Akbar, Jahangir and Shah Jahan, popularized a style of painting where small paintings, usually part of books, were made. These tiny but highly detailed paintings are called ☐☐☐☐☐☐☐☐☐ paintings.

4. Kishangarh is a small town in the desert state of ☐☐☐☐☐☐☐☐☐ known for the same kind of painting.

5. The ☐☐☐☐☐☐ style of painting, whose name comes from the Hindi word for mountain, was largely based in the historic town of Kangra in Himachal Pradesh.

6. This lovely painting is one of hundreds made by ☐☐☐☐ ☐☐☐☐ ☐☐☐☐☐, an artist from Kerala, who is well known for depicting gods and goddesses.

7. This is a self-portrait by _ _ _ _ _ _ _ _ _ _ _ _ _, of Indo-Hungarian parentage.

8. This painting is in the Kalighat Style from _ _ _ _ _ _. One of the most famous artists of this style was Jamini Roy.

9. This painting of horses was made by _ _ _ _ _ _ _ _ _ who is considered among the greatest of modern Indian painters.

10. _ _ _ _ _ art, created with white paste made from rice and water, is named after the group of tribal people who make these paintings.

11. _ _ _ _ _ _ _ paintings, which are known for their use of gold paint and semi precious stones, are named after a town, also called Thanjavur, in Tamil Nadu.

12. _ _ _ _ _ _ _ _ _ is a centuries-old style of painting from Mithila in Bihar that gets its name from the words for honey and forest.

Madhubani	Amrita Sher-gil	Pahari	Rajasthan
Ajanta	Warli	Miniature	Bengal
MF Hussain	Tanjore	Caves	Raja Ravi Varma

COOL FACT

The Constitution of India is a beautifully illustrated document. The illustrations and calligraphy (decorative writing style) were done by a team led by an eminent artist from Bengal, Nandalal Bose.

Airlines and Logos

Look at these logos. Eleven of them are logos of international airlines, while five are not. Mark the airline logos with a tick (✓) and the non-airline logos with a cross (×).

1.

2.

3.

4.

5.

6.

7.

8.

9.
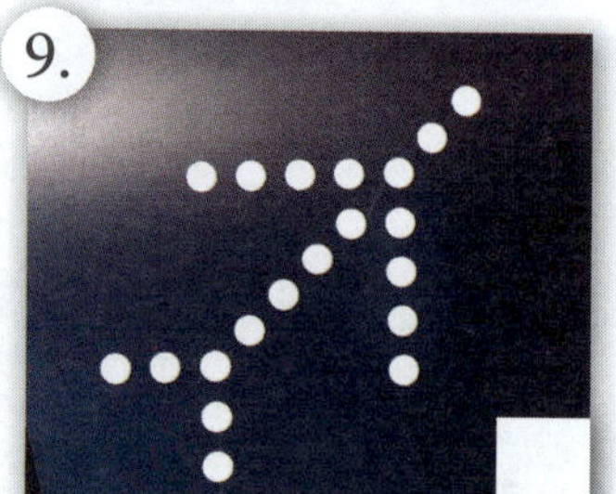

10.

11.

12.

13.

14.

15.

16.

COOL FACT

KLM or Royal Dutch Airlines is the longest, continuously-operating airline in the world. It operated its first flight in 1920.

13

Technology Decoded

Complete the five lists below. We have given three examples in each list. Find and write the other three from the help box.

1. Operating System

a. DOS b. Xenix
c. UNIX d. ____________
e. ____________ f. ____________

2. Languages

a. Visual BASIC b. Pascal
c. COBOL d. ____________
e. ____________ f. ____________

3. Browser

a. Netscape Navigator b. Internet Explorer
c. Safari d. ____________
e. ____________ f. ____________

4. Application software

a. Photoshop b. Word
c. Excel d. ____________
e. ____________ f. ____________

5. Search engine

a. Altavista b. AOL
c. Lycos d. ____________
e. ____________ f. ____________

MAC OS X	Java
PowerPoint	Chrome
Google	C
CorelDraw	Paint
FORTRAN	Yahoo
Linux	Bing
Windows 10	Firefox
Opera	

COOL FACT

Sergey Brin and Larry Page invented the search engine Google, whose name is based on googol, that is, 1 followed by 100 zeros. It is the most widely used search engine in the world.

28

Different Kinds of Boats

There are many kinds of boats. Match the boat descriptions with their pictures.

1. Boat which has a motor installed for travelling fast on water
2. Small ship which pulls a bigger ship or boat, found near the port
3. Boats with sails used for racing or recreation
4. A traditional boat of Tamil Nadu, made of logs tied together
5. Ships that moves underwater

a. 

catamaran

b. 

submarine

c. 

speedboat

d. 

tugboat

e. 

yacht

COOL FACT

A great game to help you pass time in an interesting way is the strategic pen-and-pad game called Battleship(s) or Sea Battle. Its origins go back to the First World War, and it works on a grid with squares filled to represent different ships.

29

Move Like an Animal

Animals have different body parts that help them move. In the following statements, choose and write the right option.

1. The tiger's ____________ helps it to balance when running or pouncing. (legs/head/tail)
2. Lizards have five wide ____________ on each foot that are covered with millions of tiny hairs called cilia. These create electrical forces that glue the lizard to any surface, even glass! (toe nails/toe pads/webs)
3. Snakes move by wriggling on their ____________ from side to side to form S-shaped curves that push the body forward. (scales/suction pads/backs)
4. Frogs walk and leap. They have powerful ____________ which push their body off the ground. (stomach muscles/hind legs/forelegs)
5. Camels have ____________ that help them walk easily in the desert sand without sinking in. (webbed feet/thorny soles/broad feet)
6. Snails and slugs have a single large ____________ on which they creep across the ground or along plants. (foot/tail/shell)
7. Monkeys move from branch to branch with great speed and skill through the forest canopy, using their ____________ as the fifth limb. (head/tail/tongue)
8. Bats have strong ____________ that help them in hanging upside down. (teeth/claws/wings)

COOL FACT

Thomisus telanganensis is the scientific name for the Telengana Crab Spider, discovered just in 2015. It not only looks like a crab, it also moves sideways like crabs.

30

Safety During Celebrations

Festivals are fun. India has many religious and civil festivals that we celebrate with great pomp and show. But while celebrating, we must remember that our own safety and that of our dear ones, and even that of the entire community, is very important.

Let us play a Safety Game.

Number of players : two players or teams; one Referee, if required (can be a teacher, a parent, class monitor or someone all players agree on)

You will need : some sheets of blank paper with pencils/pens
a timer (watch or phone would do)
two tokens (one per team)
dice

1. If you use chemical instead of natural or organic colours...

2. If you light oil lamps in a closed staircase...

3. If you play ball games while wearing glass bangles...

4. If you light crackers in your hand...

5. If you throw water balloons from a height...

6. If you eat too much heavy festival food...

7. If you keep large candles burning when you go out for a couple of hours...

8. If you play Holi without first applying oil or cream in your hair and on your skin...

9. If you use cheap decorative lights that end in loose wires...

Both teams throw the dice. The team with more points (let us call it Team 1) starts. The token sits on the Start Box. When the timer starts, the team has to write down all possible "Safe" endings for the half-sentence shown in the box. At the end of a minute, The Referee blows a whistle and reads all the complete sentences. For each valid full sentence, the team gets 1 point. For every invalid or incomplete sentence, it gets -1.

The other team (Team 2) then plays in the same way. The team to complete the grid with the maximum number of points wins.

To increase interest and/or redeem a one-sided game, any two times in the game, a team can challenge the other for the same Box. Within that minute, whichever team get more points adds up its score while the other gets no points on that box.

Tip : This is supposed to be a fun game that encourages us all to think of safety while celebrating. Game rules can be changed to suit every group, as long as the answers are all safety-related!

10. If you wear fancy new clothes that sweep the ground on a festival day...

11. If you hang Christmas tree ornaments when the tree lights are wound around and lit...

12. If you spend several hours in the sun while observing a Ramadan fast...

13. If you leave your parents or family members during a festive outing, such as a fair ground or place of worship...

14. If you hang paper lanterns with bulbs inside them out on a balcony in the rain...

15. If you fling a handful of dry colour on someone's face...

16. If you use metallic twine (manjha) as kite string...

Super Birds

All these birds break records in the bird kingdom. Match these super birds with their descriptions by writing the number of the description against their picture.

Barn Owl

Bee Hummingbird

Ostrich

Albatross

Snowy Owl

1. The fastest-moving bird, it can dive at over 300 km per hour.
2. The slowest-flying bird, it flies at a mere speed of 8 km per hour.
3. The most aquatic bird, this black and white bird found in the southern hemisphere spends seventy five per cent of its life in the sea.
4. This bird's wing beat is very, very slow, at barely 1 per second.
5. This bird can withstand extremely cold temperatures, lower than -60°C. It is Harry Potter's pet too.
6. This bird has the keenest sense of hearing.
7. This is the tiniest bird, measuring just a bit less than 6 cm from beak to tail. Its name includes the name of a buzzing insect.
8. This enormous flightless bird lays the biggest egg, measuring about 17 cm×11 cm.
9. This seabird is the most infrequent egg-layer. It lays a single egg once every two years.

American Woodcock

Peregrine Falcon

Vulture

Penguin

COOL FACT

The Crested Argus Pheasant has the longest tail feathers among all birds, measuring as much as 173 cm (that's about the height of an adult human being).

INDIA

32

Traditional Musical Instruments of India

Use the descriptive clues to guess the answers of the following. We have provided a help box, but watch out! There are two incorrect answers.

1. Out of which material was the bowstring of a *sarangi* traditionally made?

______

2. Which instrument, similar to the Western tambourine, consists of a circular frame made of the wood of the jackfruit tree covered on one side with a drumhead made of monitor lizard skin?

______

3. The *tutari*, still played in Maharashtra, was once used to motivate soldiers on the battlefield. What kind of instrument is it?

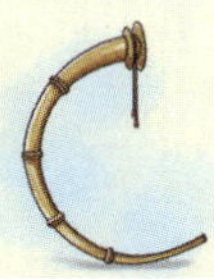

______

4. What type of instrument is the *lezeem* or the *manjeera*?

______

5. Which musical instrument has a pair of kettle drums, with the bigger one made of copper covered with buffalo skin and the smaller one made of steel and covered with camel skin?

______

6. What is the name of this traditional musical instrument, often played by snake charmers, made of wood and gourd that has three pipes but only one of them has holes for creating the various notes?

______

nagada violin horse hair *been* *kanjira* trumpet cymbals *tabla*

COOL FACT

According to Indian mythology, Ravana, the king of Lanka, played a string instrument. It is called the *Ravanhatta*, after him, and is believed to be the oldest instrument to be played with a bow.

AROUND THE WORLD

33

Let's Visit Pakistan

Pakistan is our neighbour in the North West. The name Pakistan means 'land of the pure'.

Solve this acrostic using the clues below. The central column is the site of one of the world's oldest civilisations. Its name means 'mound of the dead'.

1. The capital of Pakistan

2. An important crop grown in Pakistan

3. A province in Pakistan

4. A mountain pass that connects Pakistan with Afghanistan

5. An overseas Pakistani musician, former member of a famous boy band

6. The founder of modern Pakistan

7. Capital city of Emperor Jahangir

8. A Pakistani cricketer

9. Pop/rock singer famous in Bollywood

10. One of the principal languages of Pakistan

11. A team sport in which Pakistan has won an Olympic Gold Medal

COOL FACT

The youngest ever Nobel Prize winner is from Pakistan. 17-year old Malala Yousafzai, born in 1997, shared the Nobel Prize for Peace in 2014 along with Kailash Satyarthi, an Indian crusader for children's rights.

SPORTS

34

Rules of the Game

Match the sports with their rules. Three rules are given for each sport. But watch out! Two extra sports have been shown.

a. football

b. hockey

c. volleyball

d. table tennis

1. i. The top of the net, along its whole length, must be 15.25 cm above the playing surface. ☐
   ii. The ball is struck with a racquet, also called a bat or a paddle.
   iii. Shake hand, penhold or seemiller are the most common ways to grip the racquet.

2. i. This is the only game in this set that does not involve playing with a ball. ☐
   ii. While serving, the players stand inside the service court.
   iii. If a third game is played in a match, players change sides when the leading score is 11.

3. i. At all times in this game, each team must have five players. ☐
   ii. A successful free throw attempt shall count as one point.
   iii. Dr. James Naismith invented this game to keep children occupied during the winter.

4. i. An international game, divided into two halves of 45 minutes each.

   ii. The top goal scorer in the International World Cup wins the Golden Boot.

   iii. Only goalkeepers are allowed to touch the ball with any part of the arm.

5. i. This game has a 'field' and an 'ice' variety, played respectively with a ball and a puck.

   ii. The stick used to strike the ball does not have a 'leftie' version, unlike other games like golf.

   iii. A match of the 'field' variety of this game is divided into two halves of 35 minutes each.

6. i. This game may be played on grass, clay, synthetic turf or even concrete.

   ii. If the opposing player is unable to touch the ball on a serve, the service is called an Ace.

   iii. If both players score 40 points, it is said to be a deuce.

lawn tennis

basketball

baseball

badminton

COOL FACT The modern game of badminton used to be played by British soldiers in India and was called Poona after the city of Poona (now known as Pune). The game was renamed after Badminton Hall, Gloucestershire, England.

35

The Story of Cricket

Cricket is easily the most popular sport in India. Here is its story.

1

We can say with certainty that an early form of cricket was being played in England around 1550 AD.

2

Initially, the wicket comprised only one stump, and bats were curved—almost like hockey sticks. Bowlers rolled the ball along the ground.

3

In 1787, the Marylebone Cricket Club or MCC was formed. The rules of the modern game of cricket evolved from here on. The wicket became broader with three stumps. Bowlers began bowling 'round-arm' and then 'over-arm'.

4

The first international cricket match was played between USA and Canada at New York in 1844. The first test match was played between England and Australia at Melbourne in 1877. It was around this time that Dr. WG Grace became the first 'superstar' of cricket.

5

In 1900, cricket was played at the Olympic Games in Paris for the first and last time. India played its first test match at Lord's in 1932. This period was known for the remarkable batting feats of Don Bradman who averaged 99.94 in test cricket.

COOL FACT In a game of cricket, a batsman can get out in one of ten different ways. Can you name them all?

6

In the 1960s, one day cricket became popular in England. The first One Day International was played in 1971 between Australia and England at Melbourne.

7

The Cricket World Cup for men was first held in 1975, and has been held every four years since then. Surprisingly, the first Cricket World Cup for women was held earlier than that, in 1973.

8

India has won the World Cup twice—in 1983, under Kapil Dev's captaincy and in 2011 when Mahendra Singh Dhoni was the captain.

9

The shortest form of International Cricket is T20 Cricket, a development of the 21st Century.

10

Today cricket is played in over 100 countries worldwide.

SCIENCE

36

Freaky Inventions

Inventions can range from important things like engines, machines, television and computers to the smallest bottle cap.

Identify these common things from the descriptions. Their names are given in the help box below.

1. This invention was, at first, used to fasten boots and shoes (in place of buttons or buckles), and was invented by Whitcomb L. Judson.

____

2. In 1974, Arthur Fry invented this sticky paper note that was reusable, stuck to surfaces and when peeled off, left no trace.

____

3. In 1899, Johann Vaalerre designed this tiny thing, originally invented by Mathew Schooley, using a flat loop and 'leg'. This single piece of wire keeps papers together.

____

4. This invention was made by Walter Hunt in 1849, in just three hours. This little object, made with a piece of wire, is used the world over to clutch or grip clothes together.

____

COOL FACT

Bernard Silver and Norman Woodland invented the bar code, which is a set of thick and thin lines that can be read by an electronic scanner. The first thing to be sold using a bar code was a packet of chewing gum in 1974.

5. In 1945, Hungarian Laszlo Josef Biro used the idea of making ink flow through a tiny ball in a writing instrument and made it a practical and usable invention. It is still in use.

____

6. This invention was initially named Mistake Out, in 1951, by inventors Bette and Graham Nesmith. Known as Liquid Paper, it was used to cover up typing errors.

____

7. This invention by Marvin Chester Stone of USA, in 1886, was originally used to drink liquids using pipes made of paper.

____

8. This invention made by Johan Edvard Lundstrom, in 1855, used the stable red phosphorus to produce a quick, easy and safe way of making fire.

____

9. This invention was made, in 1955, by George de Mestral when he noticed that prickly plants called cockle burrs got temporarily caught in his dog's fur. Today, it is used to fasten shoes, clothes, bags and all kinds of things. To open, the ends are simply ripped apart.

____

velcro	ball point pen	safety pin	post-it notes	zip fastener
paper clip	correction fluid	safety matches	drinking straws	

The Fantasy World of Roald Dahl

A. *Read the six statements below and match each one with one of the Roald Dahl books given in the box. Beware! There are four extra names that do not match.*

1. The Old Green Grasshopper, the Centipede, the Earthworm, the Ladybug and the other insects live inside a huge magical fruit, and have many adventures.

   ____

2. The Oompa Loompas helped the mysterious candy maker, Willy Wonka, run his workshop.

   ____

3. Mr and Mrs Wormwood sent their brilliant daughter to a school run by the awful headmistress, Miss Trunchball.

   ____

4. A brave, young boy and his Norwegian grandmother thwart a fiendish plan to get rid of all the children of England.

   ____

5. Boggis, Bunce and Bean are three wicked farmers who are always outwitted by a clever animal who lives down a hole.

   ____

COOL FACT

Roald Dahl was a fighter pilot during World War II. That's where he got the idea for one his first children's stories, *The Gremlins*.

6. The Muggle Wumps were the pet monkeys who escaped their unkind owners with the help of the Roly-Poly Bird.

   ____

B. *Now write such statements for other Roald Dahl stories that you love and ask your friends to guess the stories.*

C. *List down your favourite Roald Dahl characters and say why you chose them.*

Matilda	*The Twits*	*Fantastic Mr. Fox*	*George's Marvellous*
The Gremlins	*The BFG*	*The Witches*	*James and the Giant Peach*
My Uncle Oswald	*Medicine*	*Charlie and the Chocolate Factory*	

What Is to What?

Bird is to fly as fish is to swim. This statement means, just as birds fly, fish swim.

A. *Here are some more expressions. Complete them.*

1. Horse is to stable as man is to __________
2. Ant is to __________ as dog is to mammal
3. Square is to four as __________ is to six
4. __________ is to pen as paint is to brush
5. Prime Minister is to country as __________ is to state

B. *Now try the same with the following.*

1. __________ is to Thames as Delhi is to Yamuna
2. Peter Parker is to Spiderman as Bruce Wayne is to __________
3. Mount Everest is to __________ as Mont-Blanc is to Alps
4. Pandit Ravi Shankar is to sitar as Ustad Zakir Hussain is to ________
5. Gateway of India is to Mumbai as __________ is to Delhi
6. USA is to The Star-Spangled Banner as India is to __________
7. Sachin Tendulkar is to cricket as Koneru Humpy is to __________
8. India is to the Tricolour as __________ is to Union Jack
9. Steve Jobs is to Apple as Bill Gates is to __________
10. Earth is to __________ as Jupiter is to Ganymede
11. Eden Gardens is to Kolkata as Chinnaswamy Stadium is to __________
12. Newton is to __________ as Einstein is to relativity

Cool Activity

Make your own expressions using facts like

- countries and capitals
- countries and sobriquets
- countries and currencies

State and Vehicle Codes

All motor vehicles have registration numbers that we can see. These number and letter combinations are actually codes to identify a vehicle. They allow the police to identify the vehicle in case it is lost or stolen.

A. *The first 2 letters of the number plate tell you the state in which the car was registered. Can you guess the states from their vehicle registration codes?*

Code	State	Code	State
1. GA		2. JH	
3. GJ		4. MH	
5. CG		6. ML	
7. PB		8. TN	
9. AS		10. UK	

B. *Do you know the registration codes of any other states? Write them here.*

1. ____________________
2. ____________________
3. ____________________
4. ____________________
5. ____________________

C. *Now let us try and decode a full registration number.*
If the number is: **DL 5C AA 6483**

- DL denotes Delhi.
- 5 denotes the district or RTO code.
- C denotes car (the kind of vehicle is not necessarily present in all states).
- AA is the series of two letters which, along with the last four numbers, allow for a unique combination number for the state.
- 6483 is the unique identification number.

D. *Now try to decode this registration number.* **DL 3S BZ 1941**
The above registration codes are only for private vehicles.

E. *Here are some special vehicles and their descriptions. Match them.*

1.

2.

3.

4.

5.

a. Vehicles belonging to foreign diplomats have white letters on a blue background with a licence plate containing the letters CD, standing for *Corps Diplomatique*.

b. UN vehicles have white letters on a blue background and contain the letters UN.

c. Private vehicles have black letters on a white background.

d. Military vehicles have a code that begins with an upward pointing arrow.

e. Commercial vehicles have black letters on a yellow background.

SPORTS

39

Olympic Symbols

For the first time ever in Olympic History, a special set of symbols called pictograms were made for each of the forty-one events featuring in the 2016 Rio Olympics held at Rio de Janeiro. The word pictogram literally means 'painted word' in Greek.

Identify and write the names of these sixteen pictograms.

1. 

2. 

3. 

4. 

5. 

6. 

7. 

8. 

9. 

10.

11.

12.

13.

14.

15.

16.

COOL FACT

The Summer Olympic Games are accompanied by the Paralympic Games where differently-abled sportspersons participate. There are another twenty-three differently coloured pictograms for the Paralympic Games as well. Here's one.

Gymnastics (Trampoline)
Synchronised Swimming
Modern Penthalon
Rhythmic Gymnastics
Archery
Diving
Sailing
Athletics
Tennis
Triathlon
Fencing
Rowing
Taekwondo
Boxing
Basketball
Beach Volleyball

40

Symbols in Computers

Your computer keyboard has keys that are not letters or numbers. They are called typographical symbols. They have interesting names and uses.

Match these eight symbols with their names and descriptions and write the correct matching letter next to each symbol.

1. An **ellipsis** is a punctuation mark used to leave out a word, sentence or any part of a text without changing its meaning.
2. 'Et' is the Latin word for 'and'. A character called **ampersand** was created by joining the letters E and T.
3. An **obelus** is used to represent one of the four main arithmetic operations.
4. A **hashtag** or **number sign** is a type of label that is now popularly used on social networking sites and micro-blogging services.
5. A **caret** is a symbol that is used in places in a document where a punctuation mark, word or phrase should be inserted.
6. The most famous application of the **at sign** can be seen in email addresses.
7. The **copyright** symbol is used to denote the legal right to the use and distribution of any original work.
8. **Asterisk** is one of the most widely used typographical symbols. It looks like a star.
9. **Underscore** is a character that is used to create visual spacing within a sequence of characters, where a white space character is not permitted. For example, email addresses and internet URLs.
10. A **tilde** is a special character that can be used to mean many things, for example, approximately in math. You would have seen this character on your computer keyboard, just below the Escape key.

@ # ÷ _ & … * © ~ ^

COOL FACT

Do you know that the @ sign has different names in different languages? It is called *xiao laoshu* in Taiwan which means 'little mouse', *apenstaartje* in The Netherlands which means 'little monkey's tail', *sobaka* in Russian which means 'dog' and *chiocciola* in Italian meaning 'snail'.

Quiz Yourself 1

1. What is a group of nightingales called?
2. Which river reaches depths of 220 metres in its lower course?
3. Which state is known as *Utkala* in the Indian national anthem?
4. Which city used to be the capital of India until 1911?
5. What popular product is made from the seeds of the Theobroma cacao plant?
6. The Indian Peninsula is surrounded by three water bodies. If Arabian Sea and Indian Ocean are two, which is the third?
7. Which body of water separates India from Sri Lanka?
8. With which profession would you associate a Self-Contained Underwater Breathing Apparatus?
9. Which is the only hill station in Rajasthan?
10. Which hill station in Madhya Pradesh is known as the Queen of Satpura?
11. Which city was the summer capital of India from 1864 to 1939?
12. Which of the Seven Wonders of the Ancient World is still surviving?
13. Which sea creature uses filtered sea water to pump nutrients through its nervous system?
14. Which Australian airline features a kangaroo in its logo?
15. Firefox, Opera and Safari are all types of ________________.
16. Which popular drink was created, in 1907, by the founder of the Jamia Hamdard University?
17. Which British author created the detective, Hercule Poirot?
18. In which Indian state, would you find the world's only floating wildlife sanctuary and national park?
19. Which judicial forum, in New Delhi, became the first institution in India to be given an exclusive PIN code?
20. What are the Olympic Games for the differently-abled called?

Quiz Yourself 2

1. Which extinct carnivorous marsupial, native to Australia, is also known as Thylacine?
2. What is the usual colour of a black box or flight recorder?
3. Which country is known as the Sugar Bowl of the World?
4. In terms of waste management, bulbs can be categorized under e-waste. True or false?
5. In 1947, Chuck Yeager, a United States Air Force pilot, became the first person to fly faster than what?
6. Which artist led a team that illustrated the original copy of the Indian Constitution?
7. Which state has a traditional string puppetry called Bommalattam?
8. What type of watercraft is able to operate underwater?
9. How do we better know Edson Arantes do Nascimento?
10. In which city would you find the iconic statue of Christ the Redeemer?
11. As of 2015, which sportsperson has won the maximum number of Olympic medals?
12. Which artist from Kerala, born in Kilimanoor Palace in 1848, is famous for paintings depicting gods and goddesses from Hindu mythology?

13. Which style of painting, from North Bihar, gets its name from the local words for honey and forest?
14. Which enormous flightless bird is known for laying the biggest eggs that can measure 17 cm X 13 cm?

15. Which part of its body help bats in hanging upside down?
16. Which sport, invented in India, was originally named 'Poona'?
17. Which country does Malala Yousafzai, the youngest ever Nobel Prize winner, hail from?

18. With which sport would you associate the terms 'shake hand' and 'pen hold'?
19. Where did India play its first test match?
20. What object was invented by Walter Hunt in 1849?

Keys

Page 9: 1. parliament; 2. team; 3. parcel; 4. flight; 5. run; 6. raft; 7. bouquet; 8. kettle; 9. building; 10. watch; 11. hedge; 12. cast

Page 10-11: 1. Mariana Trench; 2. Caspian Sea; 3. Death Valley; 4. Antarctica; 5. Amazon; 6. Northeast Greenland; 7. Vostok Station; 8. Mawsynram; 9. Angel; 10. Congo

Page 12-13: 1. a, iii; 2. g, vii; 3. b, i; 4. e, v; 5. b, viii; 6. f, iv; 7. c, ii; 8. h, vi

Page 14-15: 1. scuba diver; 2. astronaut; 3. clown; 4. magician; 5. weaver; 6. potter; 7. artist; 8. actor; 9. cartoonist; 10. tea taster

S	C	U	B	A	D	I	V	E	R	R	T
U	L	P	U	R	J	O	T	A	B	N	Q
N	O	E	T	T	H	A	S	S	E	E	U
N	W	R	T	I	K	C	E	T	S	S	I
Y	N	C	E	S	B	T	B	M	T	S	Z
R	A	A	S	T	R	O	N	A	U	T	M
A	C	R	R	O	E	R	L	G	N	A	A
I	K	T	L	O	Z	U	P	I	D	D	S
S	P	O	T	T	E	R	C	C	E	D	T
E	O	O	I	O	X	P	E	I	R	S	E
U	S	N	C	A	C	W	E	A	V	E	R
N	T	I	K	S	V	A	S	N	A	L	E
D	I	S	E	T	B	R	R	T	T	E	S
E	O	T	E	A	T	A	S	T	E	R	T

Cool Quiz quizmaster

Pages 16-17: A. 1. parantha, b; 2. pakora, c; 3. pulao, a; 4. kheer, f; 5. daal, d; 6. idli, e

Page 18-19: Bihar 1, 5, 9; Jharkhand 2, 6, 10; Odisha 4, 7, 12; West Bengal 3, 8, 11

Page 20: 1. black; 2. white; 3. blue; 4. red; 5. red; 6. blue; 7. white; 8. black; 9. white; 10. red; 11. black; 12. blue

Page 21: A. Across 2. lonely; 5. generous; 8. frugal; 9. gloomy; 10. radiance Down 1. undress; 3. laughable; 4. hurry; 6. eyeball; 7. critical
B. King Lear; Macbeth; Hamlet; Othello

Page 22: A.
1. Baisakhi; 2. Gudi Padwa; 3. Naba Barsha; 4. Navreh; 5. Ugadi; 6. Vishu; 7. Thapna

Cool Activity 1. Tamil Nadu; 2. Manipur; 3. Assam

A	C	E	V	O	B	M	G	T	U
G	U	D	I	P	A	D	W	A	P
A	P	I	S	N	I	Y	E	S	P
G	P	S	H	O	S	B	S	T	E
A	T	T	U	G	A	D	I	Y	R
M	H	R	X	Z	K	E	T	T	E
N	A	V	R	E	H	S	E	N	S
E	P	I	E	R	I	T	U	W	T
O	N	C	S	T	N	O	P	Q	O
N	A	B	A	B	A	R	S	H	A

Page 23: 1. a; 2. a; 3. b; 4. b; 5. b; 6. a; 7. b; 8. a

Page 24-25: A. 1. e; 2. b; 3. a; 4. c; 5. d; 6. h; 7. g; 8. f
B. 1. Milky Bar; 2. Munch; 3. Five Star; 4. Bournville; 5. Perk; 6. Kitkat; 7. Dairy Milk; 8. Amul; 9. Mars; 10. Kinder Joy

Page 26-27: 1. Nainital, Uttarakand (given); 2. Ooty, Tamil Nadu; 3. Mount Abu, Rajasthan; 4. Matheran, Maharashtra; 5. Manali, Himachal Pradesh; 6. Gulmarg, Jammu and Kashmir; 7. Saputara, Gujarat; 8. Morni Hills, Haryana; 9. Madikeri, Karnataka; 10. Munnar, Kerala; 11. Pachmarhi, Madhya Pradesh; 12. Darjeeling, West Bengal

Page 28: 1. g; 2. f; 3. b; 4. a; 5. c; 6. d; 7. e

Page 29: A. Rupee Maldives, Mauritius, Nepal, Pakistan, Sri Lanka; Dollar Australia, Canada, Hong Kong, New Zealand, USA; Dinar Algeria, Iraq, Jordan, Kuwait, Libya B. 1. b; 2. a; 3. d; 4. c; 5. e

Page 30: 1. Indian ink; 2. Portuguese man-o'-war; 3. Turkish towel; 4. French fries; 5. Russian salad; 6. Chinese checkers; 7. Swiss knife; 8. Japanese fan; 9. Arabian mare; 10. German shepherd; 11. Persian carpet; 12. Danish Pastry

Page 31: a. 11 (given); b. 4; c. 12; d. 10; e. 1; f. 5; g. 6; h. 2; i. 7; j. 3; k. 9; l. 8

Page 32-33: A. Across 1. volcano; 3. earthquake; 4. cyclone; 6. tornado; 8. typhoon; Down 2. lightning; 5. drought; 6. tsunami; 7. flood B. 1. b; 2. c; 3. a

Page 34-35: 1. Bengal, b; 2. Goa Catholic, d; 3. Tamil Nadu, c; 4. Coorg (Karnataka), a; 5. Maharashtra, f; 6. Ladakh, g; 7. Sikh, a; 8. Uttar Pradesh, h

Page 36-37: 1, 8, 9, 3, 7, 10, 4, 5, 6, 2

Page 38-39: A. 1. e; 2. c; 3. d; 4. b; 5. a B. 1. c; 2. a; 3. e; 4. f; 5. b; 6. d; C. 1. e, iii; 2. h, x; 3. j, vi; 4. a, vii; 5. g, viii; 6. b, ii; 7. i, v; 8. c, ix; 9. d, i; 10. f, iv

Page 40-41: a. ii; b. i; c. ii; d. ii; e. i; f. ii; g. final goal; h. i; j. i; k. ii; m. ii; n. ii; q. ii; r. ii.; s. i; t. i; u. ii; v. ii; w. ii; y. i

Pages 42-43: ☺ 2, 4, 7, 8, 9 ☹ 1, 3, 5, 6, 10

Page 44-45: 1. g; 2. d; 3. k; 4. h; 5. a; 6. i; 7. c; 8. j; 9. f; 10. l; 11. b; 12. e

Page 46: 1. octopus; 2. seal; 3. jellyfish; 4. hippopotamus; 5. reindeer; 6. dolphin; 7. penguin; 8. starfish

Page 47: A. 1. c. v; 2. d. iii; 3. a. iv; 4. e. i; 5. b. ii
B. panchamrit, panchang, panchatantra, panchashila, panchayat

Page 48: 1. Arunachal Pradesh, Brahmaputra; 2. Loktak Lake; 3. Meghalaya; 4. Mizoram; 5. Mount Saramati; 6. Kanchenjunga; 7. Tripura

Page 49: A. 1. China; 2. Japan; 3. France; 4. Italy; 5. Russia; 6. Brazil; 7. Canada; 8. Australia; 9. New Zealand; 10. Pakistan B. 1. Democratic Republic of the Congo; 2. Tuvalu; 3. Federated States of Micronesia; 4. Djibouti; 5. Montenegro; 6. Mauritius

Pages 50-51: 1. 517352; 2. 731204; 3. 400001; 4. 171001; 5. 110011; 6.362268

Page 52-53: 1. f, v; 2. e, iii; 3. d, vi; 4. c, i; 5. b, iv; 6. a, ii

Page 54: 1. rising sun; 2. playground; 3. sugar bowl; 4. tulips; 5. thunderdragon; 6. white elephant; 7. maple leaf; 8. rainbow; 9. gift; 10. long white cloud

Page 55: 1. fifth, South, Chile; 2. Sao Paulo, Beach, Christ, Sugar Loaf; 3. Amazon, rainforest, piranha; 4. carnival; 5. coffee; 6. football, Pele; 7. lambada

Page 56-57: 1. Labrador; 2. Poodle; 3. Pug; 4. Golden retriever; 5. Pomeranian; 6. Dalmatian; 7. German Shepherd; 8. St. Bernard

Page 58-59: A. 1. a, c, g, j, k, p, q; 2. b, e, h, l, o, r, u; 3. d, f, i, m, n, s, t B. ☺ 1, 5, 6, 7, 8

Page 60-61: 1. T; 2. F; 3. T; 4. T; 5. F

Page 64-65: 1. c, v; 2. a, iv; 3. b, i; 4. e, ii; 5. d, iii; 6. i, vii; 7. j, vi; 8. f, x; 9. h, viii; 10. g, ix

Page 66-67: 1. caves; 2. Ajanta; 3. Miniature; 4. Rajasthan; 5. Pahari; 6. Raja Ravi Varma; 7. Amrita Sher-gil; 8. Bengal; 9. MF Hussain; 10. Warli; 11. Tanjore; 12. Madhubani

Page 68: Non-airline logos 1. India Post; 3. Maersk; 6. Amtrak; 12. DHL (operates international cargo airline); 15. National Express

Page 69: Operating System Linux, MAC OS X, Windows 10; Languages Java, FORTRAN, C; Browsers Firefox, Chrome, Opera; Application Software PowerPoint, CorelDraw, Paint; Search Engine Google, Yahoo, Bing

Page 70: 1. c; 2. d; 3. e; 4. a; 5. B

Page 71: 1. tail; 2. toe pads; 3. scales; 4. hind legs; 5. broad feet; 6. foot; 7. tail; 8. claws

Page 72-73 (indicative list only): 1. your skin could break out into rashes/the colour may not come off easily/the colour could cause allergies/ the colour could stick to nails or hair; 2. the smoky carbon monoxide gas that is released could choke you/ the flame of the lamps could spread and cause a bigger fire/ short circuit/ people or their belongings may get burnt 3. the bangles could break and the glass could cut your wrist, arm, foot or other body part or injure someone else; 4. they could explode on you or another person and cause a lot of damage; 5. you could hurt/ injure people badly; 6. you could have a bad stomach upset; 7. the candles might tip over and cause a fire or short circuit; 8. the colour may stick to your hair or skin and removal could be painful/ the colour could cause rashes or dryness; 9. the loose wires could cause an electrical short circuit or even fire/ they may even blow the entire power supply of your home out/ you could get an electric shock; 10. your clothes could catch fire if there are crackers or lamps on the ground/ your clothes could get badly soiled, as there is often spilt food, oil or other things on festivals; 11. you could get a bad electric shock if you touch any loose or hanging wire; 12. you could get sunstroke or dehydration; 13. you could get lost in the crowds and might not be able to find your way home; 14. the water could cause an electrical short circuit or a fire/ the wet wall could give you an electric shock if you touch it; 15. the colour could go into their eyes and be painful/the colour could fly into someone else's or even your own eyes; 16. you could injure yourself or someone else very badly, or worse, cut off someone's neck, as metallic twine is very sharp and very dangerous

Page 74: 1. Peregrine Falcon; 2. American Woodcock; 3. Penguin; 4. Vulture; 5. Snowy Owl; 6. Barn Owl; 7. Bee Hummingbird; 8. Ostrich; 9. Albatross

Page 75: 1. horse hair; 2. kanjira; 3. trumpet; 4. cymbals; 5. tabla; 6. been

Page 76-77: 1. Islamabad; 2. cotton; 3. Sindh; 4. Khyber; 5. Zayn Malik; 6. Jinnah; 7. Lahore; 8. Shahid Afridi; 9. Atif Aslam; 10. Urdu; 11. hockey Acrostic Mohenjo Daro

Page 78-79: 1. d; 2. h; 3. f; 4. a; 5. b; 6. e

Page 82-83: 1. zip fastener; 2. post-it notes; 3. paper clip; 4. safety pin; 5. ball point pen; 6. correction fluid; 7. drinking straw; 8. safety matches; 9. velcro

Page 84: A. 1. James and the Giant Peach; 2. Charlie and the Chocolate Factory; 3. Matilda; 4. The Witches; 5.Fantastic Mr. Fox; 6. The Twits

Page 85: A. 1. house; 2. insect; 3. hexagon; 4. ink; 5. Chief Minister B. 1. London; 2. Batman; 3. The Himalayas; 4. tabla; 5. India Gate; 6. Jana Gana Mana; 7. chess; 8. United Kingdom; 9. Microsoft; 10. Moon; 11. Bangalore/ Bengaluru; 12. Gravity

Page 86-87: A. 1. Goa; 2. Jharkhand; 3. Gujarat; 4. Maharashtra; 5. Chhattisgarh; 6. Meghalaya; 7. Punjab; 8. Tamil Nadu; 9. Assam; 10. Uttarakhand E. 1. c; 2. e; 3. d; 4. b; 5. A

Page 88-89: 1. Archery; 2. Gymnastics (Trampoline); 3. Tennis; 4. Synchronised Swimming; 5. Rowing; 6. Athletics; 7. Rhythmic Gymnastics; 8. Basketball; 9. Fencing ; 10. Sailing; 11. Boxing; 12. Triathlon; 13. Taekwondo; 14. Modern Pentathlon; 15. Beach Volleyball; 16. Diving

Page 90: 1. ...; 2. &; 3. ÷; 4. #; 5. ^; 6. @; 7. ©; 8. *; 9. _; 10. ~

Page 91: 1. Watch; 2. Congo; 3. Odisha; 4. Kolkata (Calcutta); 5. Chocolate; 6. Bay of Bengal; 7. Palk Strait; 8. Diver ; 9. Mount Abu; 10. Pachmarhi; 11. Simla; 12. Pyramids of Giza; 13. Starfish; 14. Qantas; 15. Browsers; 16. Rooh Afza; 17. Agatha Christie; 18. Manipur; 19. Supreme Court of India; 20. Paralympics

Page 92: 1. Tasmanian Tiger or Tasmanian Wolf; 2. Orange; 3. Cuba; 4. True; 5. Sound; 6. Nandlal Bose; 7. Andhra Pradesh; 8. Submarine; 9. Pele; 10. Rio de Janeiro; 11. Michael Phelps; 12. Raja Ravi Varma; 13. Madhubani; 14. Ostrich; 15. Claws; 16. Badminton; 17. Pakistan; 18. Table Tennis; 19. Lord's; 20. Safety Pin